Another Long Hot Soak

BOOK THREE

Over 50 Stories to
Warm the Heart
and Inspire the Spirit

Edited by **Chris Gidney**

ZONDERVAN™

GRAND RAPIDS, MICHIGAN 49530 USA

ZONDERVAN™

Another Long Hot Soak – Book Three
Copyright © 2003 by Chris Gidney and Guideposts, Carmel, New York 10512

Requests for information should be addressed to:
Zondervan, *Grand Rapids, Michigan 49530*

The author asserts the moral right to be identified as the compiler of this work.

ISBN 0-310-25177-X

Printed in the United States

05 06 07 08 09 10 /❖DCI/ 10 9 8 7 6 5 4 3

CONTENTS

Introduction by Chris Gidney   9

1. When Angels Move Amongst Us

Ten Minutes To Live by Dennis Jodouin   13
Silent Hands by Mary Hattan Bogart   18
Wreck in the Storm by Dan Kulchytsky   20
Visitor on Our Doorstep by Arthur Best   24
Desert Rescue by Michael Toth   29
Figures Amid the Flames by Debra Faust   31
The Mysterious Man by Laura S. Curran   35
Stranger with a Flask by Paul DeLisle   37
Mum's Angels by Jacquelin Gorman   40

2. When Love Is Re-Discovered

The Great Experiment by Tom Anderson   47
They Never Said Hello by Cecilia Reed   49
Lovers Meeting by Cindy Goss   54
A Change of Heart by Mary Simmons   59
Saving a Marriage by Arthur Gordon   64
Life Begins At 70 by Marjorie & George Holmes   66
A Christmas Crisis by Melva Smith   72
Prodigal Father by Dale Kugler   76
A Golden Marriage by Faye Field   79

3. When Heaven Is At Hand

Return from Tomorrow by Dr George Ritchie   83
The Awakening by Michelle Yates   88
A Stream in the Desert by Betsy Young   94
Out of Our Hands by Roy Gilliland   96
A Glimpse of Heaven by Janet Franck   99
Lost in the Whirlpool by Donald Shaffer   104
No Longer Afraid by Linda Hanick   109
The Gateway by Martin Bauer   111
Here for Good by Grace Dodds   116
Strong and Free by Lois Lemieux   120

4. When Families Can Be Fun

Motorized Mother by Patricia Lorenz   127
Love Without Smothering by Danny Kaye   130
Don't Give Up by Marjorie Holmes   133
Joe Goes to Disneyland by Lois Woods   138
The Case of the Longhaired Son by Phyllis Malone   142
Families Can Be Better by Margaret Peale   147
Alone Through the Dark by Ruth Hagen   150
Teen for a Day by Karen Barber   154
The Knock At My Door by Claudia Leaman   158

5. When Honesty Is the Best Policy

Adventures of a Pen Pal by Myrtle Potter   165
Truth is Good Business by David Schwartz   169
I'll Never Forget by Calvin Fudge   175
Everybody Does It by Jack Griffin   179
An Agonizing Decision by Sidney Fields   181
Words to Grow On by Walter Cronkite   186
That Toothpaste Smile by Austin Colgate   188

6. When Dreams Come True

The Dream That Wouldn't Go Away by George Hunt   193

A Giant Beside Our House by Ron Gullion   197

The Pin by Mary Rosco   203

Recurring Dream by June Davis   205

A Dream Come True by Norman Vincent Peale   206

A Voice in the Blizzard by Vance Thurston   208

Heaven Is for Dancing by Catherine Marshall   213

Where to Find Help   216

INTRODUCTION

by Chris Gidney

Words are incredibly powerful things.

Recently I have been struck by how much influence the written or spoken word can have on a person's life. 'Sticks and stones will break my bones, but words will never hurt me.' This little verse, hastily spewed by kids from kindergarten to Sunday school, must contain one of the greatest lies of all time. There can't be anybody left on planet Earth who knows that nothing brings more pain than a word uttered in hate. One sentence can cut like a knife into your confidence, your mind and your heart. This slow-release poison can even stay with you for years, affecting your life, your work and your deepest sense of faith.

As someone who has lived and worked in the entertainment business for some while, I know what it is like to be on the receiving end of a first-night critic who succeeds in dismantling six weeks of hard rehearsal in one sentence. Many in the profession now refuse to read the daily newspapers because of the destructive power they have brought into their lives.

Of course, the arrows that hurt the most are the ones that come from those closest to you. That trusted friend who releases a sudden word of jealousy quickly throws you off balance, and ruins the exhilaration you felt earlier. One word can bring you down from the mountain top into a state of dejection quicker than the new Japanese tourist attraction that drops you 300 feet inside a steel lift in under 4 seconds. It leaves your stomach in your mouth and your brain shocked and disorientated.

Is it any wonder then that God puts so much emphasis on words and their power? One of my favourite verses in the Bible comes from the New Testament, which simply says: 'Let us encourage one another. . .' Our creator intended words to build up, not to knock down.

It is interesting to see that God did not create the world with a magic wand, or a quick wave of the hand. He used his words. In the first chapter of Genesis it says that each time he spoke, something wonderful was brought to life. The sky, the oceans, the birds, the great creatures of the sea, all came to their being through his almighty word. Then God sat back for a moment and said that what he had created was 'good', until he made mankind and then he said it was 'very good'. That's where you and I come in.

Today, words are still as potent, and we have choices to make as to how we use our mouths every minute of the day. In the following stories, we can see how words have changed and shaped people's lives for the better. Whether through a simple kindness or supernatural occurrence the effect remains the same, as the old proverb announces: 'a word aptly spoken is like apples of gold in settings of silver.' I'm certain these inspirational stories will encourage you in your own journey down the often bumpy road of life.

1

WHEN ANGELS MOVE AMONGST US

Remember to welcome strangers . . .
There were some who did that and
welcomed angels without knowing it

New Testament

TEN MINUTES TO LIVE

by Dennis Jodouin

The fire was so strong it had ignited the plaster.

I used to think I was lucky. As a lieutenant in the fire service I've had water-laden ceilings fall on my head, I've been blown down by explosions, I've fallen through floors eaten by fire. But after 5 December 1984, I've had to question how much was really luck. Maybe my mother was right when she told us children that each of us had his own guardian angel.

At Engine House No. 19 on that particular December morning, we checked our equipment as usual, paying special attention to our facemasks. Smoke is the fire fighter's principal enemy, and we always make sure every valve is working, every air tank full. Then, at 10.43, the alarm sounded. As our fire engine raced to the call at a well-known department store, I wondered if everyone had got out safely. If they had, our job was to try to save the building. Our truck approached the corner. Other fire engines were laying down hoses from a hydrant, their crews stretching the lines to the front and rear of the frame duplex. Just as we pulled up, a violent back-draft explosion blew out the building's storefront window. Glass flew onto the crumbling concrete stoop.

Black, rolling smoke vented from the hole. I ordered my crew to mask up.

We were beginning to pull the hose off the engine when the chief ran over to me.

'Get upstairs quick, Lieutenant!' he said. 'Use the back way. There's been screaming reported coming from up there.'

Now it was a different ball game: We were no longer just fighting a fire, we were looking for a person trapped inside. I looked around at our new man, Bill.

'Let's go,' I said. On the way, because he was new to the job, I briefed him. We'd climb the outside stairs, gain entrance to the second floor and feel our way through the smoke in the upstairs apartment, looking for a survivor. 'Remember your training now,' I said, not thinking that within moments I'd forget my own seventeen years of experience.

We raced up the outside stairs to the landing, paused, slipped on the face-pieces of our masks and turned on the valves. There was a hiss as compressed air flowed from the tank on my back through the tube into my mask. We would have about twenty minutes before the air gave out.

'Okay, stay close to me,' I said to Bill, my voice sounding muffled as it came through the mask's speaking diaphragm. We headed inside.

The first room we came to was filled with black, black smoke. I switched on my hand light. It didn't begin to penetrate the darkness. Following procedure, I started moving to my right, feeling my way around the wall. A stove, a refrigerator and then an empty space. A doorway!

'Wait,' I said, talking into the smoke. I could hardly see Bill. We stopped and listened, but the only sound was the muffled noise of fire fighters from the street below.

Our proper procedure was clear. Crouching into a semi-crawl, we went through the doorway into the room off the kitchen, keeping contact with the wall on our right. I kept locating the wall with my foot, and then I stretched into the middle of the room feeling for a human form. I touched pieces of furniture: a sofa, a chair, and a cabinet. Then, on the floor, a heap of clothes. Was that a body? No, just clothes.

A bright blur ahead. A window. With the butt of my hand light

I burst the glass; a surge of black smoke rushed past me into the open. I kept on. Wheeze. Wheeze. I could hear Bill behind me, drawing air into his mask.

Perspiration was running in a steady stream down my face and neck, stinging my eyes. The intense heat on my neck was a constant reminder that the fire was getting closer, racing up inside the walls. I skirted a bookcase, came to a corner, turned left, following the wall. Inch by inch I groped in the darkness, searching for what, I didn't know. Except for our own wheezing breath I hadn't heard a sound in the apartment since we began the search. Now little orange fragments started falling from the ceiling. Bad news. The fire was so hot it had ignited the plaster. Bits and pieces of it were floating down from the ceiling like deadly fireflies. I touched the wall again. Even through my gloves it was hot. We had to hurry!

Suddenly I wasn't getting enough air. I inhaled more deeply. My tank couldn't be empty – we hadn't been in the building 10 minutes. The warning bell in my equipment hadn't rung. I remembered procedure, reached for the emergency bypass valve and cranked it two turns.

Nothing.

'Bill,' I yelled into the blackness, 'I've got trouble with my air.' I tried to keep my muffled voice calm, but I heard a trace of panic in it. Without air, I had one, at the most two, minutes to live.

And then I made my first mistake. I did something totally against procedure: I ignored the first rule of safety for the fire fighter – use the buddy system. In an emergency, you can share your partner's supply of air until you are out of danger.

Instead I ordered the rookie fireman away. 'Go back the way we came and get me another tank,' I shouted. 'I'll meet you at the landing.'

Bill had scarcely left when I began to choke. Now panic took an iron hold and I made my second mistake. My only thought was to get air. The quickest way was to go straight to the door without circling the wall, as I should have done. I stood up and ran.

I bumped into a table. A sofa. Another table. I ran forward, hit a chair, turned back, grasped my valve and turned it again. Nothing. My lungs burned. I sucked harder but there was just no air. Where was that door! Words came from training: 'Don't forget,' the drill instructors had preached, 'you always have air trapped inside your clothing.'

Gasping, I fell to the floor, disconnected my inhalation tube from the oxygen tank and stuck it inside my coat. Praying. A few more moments of life. Let there be air inside my fire coat!

I sucked hard. A precious bit of air came through! The smoke tasted hot, acrid, but the air was still breathable. I had bought another minute. I forced myself back up onto my hands and knees and started crawling through the obstacle course, under a table, over a stuffed chair. There was no way out now and I knew it. I started crying.

With the same strange logic I had used in sending Bill away, I blamed God for my mistakes. Over and over the thought repeated itself, irrationally, insistently, 'Dear God, why are you doing this to me? You know I'm getting married soon. I have so much to live for!'

Then I heard the voice, a whisper, 'Look up! Look up!'

I barely moved my head, turning to the right. The voice came again, more insistently, 'Not to your right, look to your left!'

The voice came more clearly now, as if through a megaphone in my ear, pressuring me as I felt my reactions slowing down. 'To your left. Look up to your left! Don't you see it?'

Yes, I saw it! Through the blackness I barely made out a small fuzzy zone of light.

In slow motion I got up and started toward it, stumbling, falling. The light became a faint outline, then a distinct form. It was a window. The same window I had broken earlier.

I ripped off my mask and forced my body halfway through the frame into the fresh air outside. Again and again I drew clean air into my lungs, relishing the sounds of men below.

Then Bill was at my side. He helped me down the stairs to the street, where I learned that the trouble with my equipment was a faulty valve. The cry from inside the building had been a cat, which had not escaped. But not one person's life was lost – including my own!

When my mother used to tell me about my guardian angel, she suggested he would stay with me always, even when, as an adult, I may forget to look up to God. Today that is a fact I no longer question. I am satisfied it was my own angel who whispered to me, 'Look up!'

SILENT HANDS

By Mary Hattan Bogart

Six mysterious strangers bring rescue.

In the late 1940's my husband, Frank, and I were driving late at night on a deserted road in the mountains near Chattanooga when we had a flat tyre. Because of the rocky road edge, Frank was unable to use the car jack and change the tyre. Out of the night a car appeared. Two of the biggest, roughest-looking bearded men I'd ever seen got out. With powerful hands they steadied the car, changed the tyre, and drove off.

They had not uttered a word.

In 1952, Frank was a Naval officer stationed in Europe. We were driving with our family through thick fog in the Swiss Alps when a gap in the road, about six feet wide and four feet deep, confronted us. Night was coming on, so Frank walked the others down to the next village. Since all our belongings were in the car, I stayed behind. I waited. Nervously I tried to pray. The words of a familiar Psalm I had learnt at Sunday school came to mind. 'God will put his angels in charge of you, to protect you wherever you go. They will hold you up in their hands. . .'

'Lord, send some of your angels please.'

A truck suddenly appeared. Out of it piled six big, rough-looking bearded men. Without speaking, they picked up their truck and carried it across the crevice. Then, with strong, powerful hands they picked up my car with me in it – carried it across the trench,

18

and set it safely on the other side. They never said a word, and disappeared into the night.

I drove into the village of Brig, where I found my family. Nobody in the village could imagine who those men were. All I knew was that they had come, and they had literally held me 'up with their hands'.

Who are these silent men? Will they have reason to help us again?

WRECK IN THE STORM

by Dan Kulchytsky

Two sailors cling to life as all hope for rescue fades.

'Look, Dad!' I pointed to a pair of elegant white swans swimming in the harbour. In more than twenty-five years of sailing on lakes, we'd seen ducks, geese and thousands of albatross – but never swans. We couldn't take our eyes off them. Their grace and beauty were mesmerizing, and they shimmered luminously in the low afternoon sun of an autumn day. Dad and I were preparing our seventeen-foot sloop *Orysia* for a short cruise around one of the biggest, and most favourite, of all our lakes.

We watched the swans a few minutes longer and then got under way, leaving the harbour about one o'clock with everything ship-shape. The wind was moderate, and *Orysia* cut cleanly through the waves as I handled the tiller. 'We could make it all the way across the lake on a day like this,' Dad said, smiling. Lake Michigan is more than a hundred miles wide.

We rounded the top of Rock Island from the west, sailing right on course. Heading south, Dad called, 'The winds are shifting. We'll have to tack.' The smooth lake surface was soon as rough as a washboard. The temperature fell rapidly. *Orysia's* sails snapped like whips. Around three o'clock, when we finally cleared the east side, reaching the passage between Rock and Washington islands, the wind had become fierce. It angled off the cliffs, blowing the water into powerful whirlpools.

20

'Get her into the wind!' Dad shouted. 'I'll get the jib and main-sail down!'

'I'll start the motor,' I yelled.

But the wind and current were too strong. Our little boat shuddered, listing to port. With a lurch and a splash of foam, the top of the mast hit the water. We were hurled against the gunwales.

'Hold on!' I cried. Too late! Dad and I were catapulted into the lake, and *Orysia*, with a final heave, capsized, her proud sails plunging into the water.

I grasped the boat's hull, trying to keep myself afloat. The water was so cold it hurt to the bone. 'Dad?' I called, looking around frantically. I felt a tug at my sleeve, and Dad surfaced beside me, gasping for air. I pulled myself up on the hull and reached for him. We flopped onto the boat, clutching the keel and shivering violently, our sodden clothing clinging to us. Then a wave surged against the boat and threw me off. 'Dad!'

Holding fast to the keel with one hand, my father thrust out his other towards me. Churning waves buffeted *Orysia*, and Dad lost his grip. He slid back into the freezing water, pulling me down with him. We clawed our way back up until we were able to grab the boat's keel again.

The winds drove us out into the huge 20,000-square-mile lake. The boat was sinking. Less than a foot of it remained above the surface. Waves crashed over us as we drifted farther from land. Then, below us, we felt the mast smash against a rocky shoal. The impact tossed us back into the water. We could only watch in horror as *Orysia's* keel disappeared into its housing beneath the waves.

A small part of the hull was still above water, but how would we hold on? Swimming to shore through the turbulent waves was an impossibility. I was almost ready to give up, almost ready to sink into the lake along with the keel. But then I felt Dad's arm around me. He pushed me toward *Orysia*. We both grabbed on and scrambled up, gripping with numb fingers the slot in the hull where the keel had been. Our bodies curved against the bulbous surface, more in the freezing water than out. We hadn't seen any other boats since we had entered the passage, and none would venture forth now in howling winds. There is no hope for us, I thought, looking at Dad.

As night fell we turned to prayer. Together and separately, aloud and silently, Dad and I asked that our lives be spared, that God would send help. When the moon rose I was able to see my watch: eight o'clock. We'd been in the lake for five hours. We talked, trying to keep alert, but our speech became slurred. I knew that meant one thing: Deadly hypothermia was setting in. I'd been cold for so long I began to have feelings of warmth. 'Keep moving,' Dad urged. We tried shifting our arms, shaking our legs, anything to keep our circulation going.

The full moon cast an eerie glow on the pitching waters. I checked my watch again. Nearly midnight. Nine hours. Our prayers for rescue changed to prayers for mercy. Death seemed imminent.

Suddenly we heard whirring above us. A searchlight cut through the blackness, reflecting off the waves. A helicopter! 'Here!' I shouted, with the little strength I had left. 'Here!' Dad echoed, even more weakly than I. We both shouted again, but the roar of the helicopter smothered our cries. The searchlight moved to our right, then to our left, but never shone on us. Abruptly the chopper flew off. The lake is so big. How will they ever see us? We're two specks down here.

The helicopter made another pass. We yelled with everything we had left. It flew on, returning several times until I couldn't yell anymore. Dad and I were exhausted. The boat had sunk lower, and we had to lift our heads out of the water just to breathe.

Then I became aware of something to the north of us. I strained to see. I saw white wings. A mirage? No, it was swans! Two swans, just as we'd seen the day before in the harbour – floating on the waves in the moonlight, their long necks swaying in a mysterious dance. What were they doing way out here?

'Dad!' My father raised his head. The swans were so beautiful we almost forgot our predicament, and as we watched I saw another searchlight sweeping towards us. A boat! But our hopes plummeted when the light shone away from us. Dad lowered his head, sighing deeply. 'No!' I screamed. Almost as if I had been heard, the light swung in our direction again. 'Look,' I said, helping my father lift his head. 'They're coming back!' The powerful beam shot out from the boat's bridge, surrounding us in its glow. We'd been found. Quickly we were hauled on board.

'We were going to head the other way,' the fishing tug's skipper told us. 'Then we thought we saw two swans in the light.' When they looked again, the swans were gone, and they spotted Dad and me instead. The two of us knew the swans had been there on the storm-tossed lake, guided by a merciful force greater than nature itself.

VISITOR ON OUR DOORSTEP

by Arthur Best

An unexpected visitor brings life.

The old country doctor set his black bag on the bedside table. 'I'm sorry, ma'am,' he said. 'I'm afraid your boy isn't going to make it through the night. A blue baby and a month and a half premature, at that . . .' His words trailed off.

Exhausted from the difficult birth, Beth nodded and leaned back against her pillows. Compared to her older sons and daughter, who had been sturdy newborns, this baby looked frail and helpless. Beth knew the boy's chances were slim at best. Besides, if an emergency arose, she and her husband, Carl, wouldn't be able to get medical help fast enough, living as they did up a hillside several miles from the nearest town. Their farm lay along a creek, and the only way coming or going was a dusty dirt road.

The doctor cleared his throat. 'I have to take your baby with me,' he said. 'The next twenty-four hours are critical. If he makes it. I'll bring him back tomorrow afternoon.' The doctor picked up the baby and carefully settled him inside the black medical bag.

Beth bit her lip, watching her boy being swallowed up by the worn leather satchel, tiny as he was. 'Thank you. Doctor,' she said, the softness of her voice matching the quiet of that spring day in 1933. 'We're grateful.'

Carl saw the doctor to the door, and then returned to his wife's bedside. 'Doctor will take good care of him,' he reassured her. He held Beth's hand, his work-roughened fingers gently curling around hers. 'All we can do is pray.'

'I know,' she whispered, her eyes half closed. 'I already am...' She drifted off to sleep.

The next day the whole family – Beth, Carl and their three older children – anxiously awaited the good doctor's arrival. Beth napped fitfully, her thoughts constantly returning to her sickly baby. When a knock finally came at the door, Carl ran to open it.

'Your boy survived the night,' the doctor said, 'although I can't quite say how.' He lifted the baby out of his bag and placed the tiny bundle in Beth's arms. The boy still looked alarmingly small, but at least he had a little colour.

'Get some milk in him,' the doctor instructed. 'And keep him warm. He seems to be allergic to cow's milk, but you shouldn't have any trouble if you nurse him.' Beth nodded, feeling reassured.

Not long after the doctor left, the baby awakened with a weak mew. 'Are you hungry?' Beth murmured, and began to nurse him. She was glad to see he had a healthy appetite. He drank his fill and nodded off, seemingly content. But before long, he began to bawl. 'What's the matter, little one?' Beth asked, gently rubbing his back. The baby promptly brought up nearly all he had consumed. Maybe he drank too fast, she thought. I'll make sure he takes it slower next time.

The next time – in fact, every time – she nursed him, produced the same dreadful results. By nightfall, she was desperate. 'He's never going to get stronger if he can't hold his milk down,' she told her husband. Remembering the doctor's admonition to keep the baby warm, she put him in a woven basket, blanket and all, and slipped him beside the kitchen stove.

The following day brought no change in the baby. Beth continued to feed him, hoping he'd keep enough in his stomach for nourishment. By late afternoon, he was whimpering constantly, whether from hunger or from illness, Beth couldn't tell. She and her husband agreed: It was time to find the doctor.

As Carl laced up his boots, a faint knock came at the door. Had the doctor decided to stop by? Eagerly Carl flung the door open.

'Doc, we were just –' He stopped short, surprised, when he saw the stranger standing there.

Unfamiliar people had stopped on their doorstep before. During those hard times, folks were walking around everywhere, looking for work in exchange for a hot meal and a place to sleep. But this woman was different. She was black. In this rural area, there were very few black people, and they always kept to themselves.

'Do you think you could let me have something to eat,' she asked, 'and maybe a place to stay? It'll only be until I get my strength back. I had a baby yesterday and I'm just too tired to go on.' When she saw the question in Carl's expression, she added, 'My child was stillborn.'

'I'm sorry,' Carl replied, beckoning her in. He led her to the rocking chair in front of the stove, where his wife sat trying to soothe the baby. 'I'm Carl Best, and this is my wife, Beth. Beth, this is – '

'Jane. Just call me Jane,' the woman said. 'I promise I'll earn my keep.'

'Now I've got to fetch the doctor,' Carl said. 'My wife will show you where you can stay.' He hurried out, and Beth explained the situation with the baby.

'I can see you have your hands full,' Jane said, gazing sympathetically at the boy in Beth's arms. 'Let me get supper on.' While Beth sat in the rocking chair, desperately trying to quiet her newborn, Jane slowly and methodically fixed a pot of soup from beef bones and vegetables.

By the time Carl returned, the children had all been fed. 'Doc's over in the next county on an emergency,' he said, crestfallen. 'He won't be back until tomorrow at the earliest.'

'Don't worry,' Jane said. 'I have the feeling your boy will be all right.'

After settling the baby in for the night in his makeshift cradle beside the stove, Beth went to sleep, prayers swirling in her mind. *Lord, please help our child,* she pleaded. *Show us what he needs.*

She awoke feeling more hopeful. When she peeked in the basket it was empty. Their baby was nowhere in sight, and neither was Jane.

'I'm going to check around,' Carl said, trying to stay calm. Beth waited and paced by the stove. Why had they helped this woman? What if she'd run away with their baby? Finally, Beth heard her husband calling in the distance, 'I found them!' She raced to the door, relieved to see Carl with the baby.

'I found them in one of the outbuildings,' he explained. 'She was letting him nurse from her and hid because she wasn't sure how we would react.'

Beth took her son in her arms and held him close. 'Look, Carl,' she said slowly, 'her milk seems to agree with him.' It was true: The baby was sleeping peacefully no crying, no spitting up.

Carl went to get Jane. After she returned to the house, the three of them agreed on the arrangement and didn't speak of the incident again. Nor did they discuss when Jane would leave. Instead she became, in a way, part of the family.

Soon Carl was back on the job cutting timber, and the two women were busy running the household. Jane never talked much, especially about herself, and Beth wasn't one to pry. The infant grew slowly but steadily.

One morning Beth and Carl arose, expecting Jane's good morning at breakfast as usual. When she wasn't at the stove, Carl went to see if she was ill. But her bed hadn't been slept in, and her few possessions were nowhere to be found. She wasn't in the garden or anywhere else on their property.

Carl rushed to their neighbours' place down the creek and asked if they'd seen her. No one had. Not so much as a dog had barked to announce someone passing. He began wondering whether anyone had seen her arrive?

When he asked, the neighbours looked bewildered. A black woman wandering these parts would have been noticed, they assured him. The folks at the other farms Jane would have passed on the dirt road to their house didn't know what Carl was talking about either.

In the months that followed, he and Beth asked friends in other counties if they had seen a woman fitting Jane's description.

The answer was always no. It was as if the earth gave birth to her and when she left, the earth swallowed her up again.

Beth and Carl were practical folk, with their feet firmly planted on the ground, and they didn't spend a lot of time pondering the mystery of Jane's visit. But whenever they spoke of her, their eyes filled with wonder. I should know. I was that sickly baby boy and I often heard the story of how a stranger arrived from nowhere to give me the nourishment that only she could give.

DESERT RESCUE

by Michael Toth

A small child recalls his first encounter with angels.

'Why won't anyone stop to help us?' Mum asked as a car whizzed past, ignoring my sister's frantic waves.

It was almost fifty miles through the desert to the next town, and I knew there was no way the three of us could walk that. Mum didn't have a clue as to what was wrong with our car.

'Let's get in out of the sun,' Mum said. We all climbed back into the car. 'We'd better pray,' she offered.

I didn't know exactly what to pray for. An angel with a tow truck? Still, we all bowed our heads and asked God to help.

After a while, we saw a blue Toyota coming down the road. The driver pulled right up to us, as if he knew we'd be there. An older couple got out. 'We were on another highway,' the lady said, 'and we heard in our prayers that someone needed our help.'

That seemed a little weird to me. But the man was a mechanic and found out the problem right away. 'Your battery's dead. I'll take it and get it recharged.'

Then the lady handed us a bag of sandwiches and assured us that they'd be back. So we ate and waited. Sure enough, a few hours later they came back with a charged-up battery.

The old lady put her hands on Mum's cheeks and said, 'You'll be all right, Cheryl.' Then she turned to my sister and me. 'Michael and Janet,' she said, 'be good to your Mum. See that she gets home safely to Indiana.'

Then they were gone. Suddenly, it hit us. That lady had called us by name, all of us. She also knew that we were going to Indiana. But we'd never told them any of that stuff!

Surprisingly, it didn't seem all that weird to me. After all, the One who told them where we were had heard our prayers – and knew our names.

FIGURES AMID THE FLAMES

by Debra Faust

The fire fighters said it was one of the hottest fires they had ever encountered.

I was putting the final load of clothes in the drier at about 10.30 that overcast May night last year. When you have four kids at home you do a lot of washing. I was exhausted, and I figured I'd leave the folding until morning. I flipped the door shut and the dryer started with a determined rumble.

The laundry room was on the first floor of our old house, just off the living room, where my husband, Bob, sat watching television. I gave him a pat on the shoulder as I passed through. 'Goin' up,' I said as he squeezed my hand.

I made my way up the sturdy old staircase to the master bedroom, recently created by knocking down the wall between two smaller rooms. It was in the middle of a paint job. The mattress lay on the floor and much of the furniture lined the hallway. But that night I didn't mind. I just wanted to crawl into bed – wherever it was.

Alicia, 14, said good night and headed down the hall to the room she shared with her sister, Wendi, 12. The boys – Sean, 4, and Dale, 10 – shared the other bedroom. I fell asleep almost instantly to the drone of the TV coming up through the floor. I must not have been sleeping long because Bob's voice still came from downstairs when I awoke to the shock of him yelling, 'Deb, the house is on fire!'

31

I jumped up, alert but a little disoriented. I stepped into the dark, cluttered hallway to be met by the overpowering stench of burning wood and insulation. 'I can't use the phone!' Bob shouted up to me, his voice seeming to rise on a cloud of thick, billowing smoke. 'I'll run next door!'

'Hurry!' I called back. 'I'll get the kids.'

I rushed to the boys' room, 'Fire!' I shouted. 'Get up! Fire!' I grabbed little Sean, but Dale slept soundly on the top bunk. I shook him. 'Dale, get up! Fire!'

Then I shouted to the girls. Acrid smoke tumbled up the stairs, filling the hallway. My eyes stung and my chest burned. I stumbled towards my daughters' room. Everything was happening so quickly in chaos of fear and confusion. I still had Sean in my arms. 'Everybody out!' I screamed, but the words seemed to bounce back in my face in the engulfing smoke.

I met Alicia coming out of her room. She was dazed and coughing. I took her by the shoulders. 'Get Wendi,' I told her.

A horrible panic came over me. Blinded and short-winded, I went back to see if Dale was up. I could barely get enough air to shout. I bumped into Alicia again and asked about Wendi, but all she could do was gag. *Dale and Wendi must have got out.* Alicia, Sean and I felt our way to the bottom of the staircase, cringing from the heat and flames shooting out from the direction of the laundry room. Then we burst through the smoke and out onto the lawn.

I opened my eyes and gulped the sweet night air, pulling Sean and Alicia close. A sprinkling rain began to fall and it felt good on my skin. Bob ran up to us, eyes wide and searching. 'Where's Dale?' he asked. 'Where's Wendi?' I began screaming their names and looking all around me. Bob ran toward the house.

They're still inside. My babies are still inside!

'Mum,' Alicia said, 'I'm going in to find them.'

'You can't go back in,' I said, catching my breath and handing her a crying Sean. 'I'll go.'

I dashed up to the front door, where Bob was being driven back by the heat and smoke. He grabbed me. 'I couldn't get farther than the landing, even on all fours,' he gasped. 'It's no use. The fire engines will be here in a minute.'.

I fell to my knees sobbing, feeling utterly helpless. I screamed inside my heart. *Help them!* Bob and I began to yell, telling Wendi and Dale to follow our voices. My throat burned from the smoke but I kept yelling, my voice hoarse and cracked. Flames danced through the living room off to my left. I heard glass shattering and a roar like a giant blowtorch. The air itself seemed about to burst into flames. Directly in front of me I could make out the first few steps of the old stairway before it disappeared into an undulating cloud of smoke, tongues of flames lapping its sides. Where were my children?

Then, in that thick haze, two figures appeared on the stairs. They seemed unaffected in any way by the raging blaze. Such calmness glowed about them that I stopped crying. *Thank you, Lord,* I prayed, standing up. *Thank you.* A complete serenity overtook me. Time slowed, stilled.

All at once the figures were gone. One small hand pushed through the smoke. Dale! His daddy grabbed him, sweeping him into his arms. *Where is Wendi?* Then her hand emerged. I pulled her out and we fell back to the lawn, crying.

The six of us huddled together as if we would never let go, watching as our house went up in flames. Forty minutes earlier I had fallen fast asleep in my bed. Now my family and I were home-less, standing in the rain in our nightclothes. When the fire engines pulled up, we retreated to our neighbour's front porch.

The old bricks in our house held in the tremendous heat, almost like a kiln, and the fire grew quickly, consuming almost everything. One fireman who tried to get in with a hose had his face shield melted. The fire fighters said it was one of the hottest fires they had ever encountered. The investigation pointed to the drier. Apparently highly combustible lint had clogged the faulty exhaust hose. There wasn't much the fire fighters could do to save our home once the blaze began.

Neighbours came to our rescue with clothes to wear until we could buy new ones. People donated food and kept us in their prayers. We spent that first night with our pastor, then a week with friends. After another week in a motel, we were able to find an apartment. Clothing poured in, especially for the little guy Sean. The school went into high gear to replace Wendi's and Dale's instruments so they could play in a band concert that first week. We always knew we lived in a wonderful community but we found out just how wonderful our people could be. Mighty God reached out to us through the helping hands of neighbours and friends – angels each and every one.

There are earth angels and there are heavenly angels. The two magnificent figures that appeared on the fiery staircase that night were sent by God to save my children, who miraculously escaped the flames unharmed and safe.

When Wendi told me, 'Mum, someone pulled me out,' we assumed she meant Dale.

'No, Mum,' he said. 'I didn't even know she was there.' We're convinced Wendi felt the hand of an angel!

Almost immediately we began building a new home on the same site. We moved in just in time for the holidays last year. Our Christmas tree had handmade decorations from family and friends.

How thankful those holidays were! A house can always be rebuilt. God looks after families first – with angels at the ready.

THE MYSTERIOUS MAN

by Laura S. Curran

I glanced back at the man whose words had held such power.

Stephen and I held hands as the plane took off from Frankfurt, Germany, and headed east. We had left the world we knew far behind that January day in 1992. My husband and I had boarded this antiquated Russian-made aircraft en route to Sofia, Bulgaria, where we planned to adopt thirteen-month-old twin girls. Although we knew them only from photographs, we had already grown to love them. Now, after four long months, we were close to fulfilling our dream.

Fog shrouded Sofia as we approached the city. The pilot announced we would land in the small town of Plovdiv instead, 130 kilometres from Sofia, far from the hotel where representatives of the adoption agency were expecting us. Stephen saw the flash of worry cross my face and squeezed my arm.

The chaotic Plovdiv airport did nothing to ease my anxiety. Hundreds of cigarette-puffing Bulgarians pushed their way towards two overworked customs agents. We struggled to find a place in line. Everything seemed to be going against us: the language, the locale – and our luggage. Along with a small suitcase, we were carrying eleven large duffel bags full of medical supplies donated for the other children at the orphanage. I looked around frantically praying for some kind of help.

And there he was. He would have stood out anywhere, this handsome man, well dressed and carrying an expensive briefcase.

He motioned to us. 'This is your place in line,' he said in perfect English. 'Here, in front of me.' We happily complied.

The U.S. Embassy had told us that visas weren't necessary to enter Bulgaria, but the customs agent demanded to see them. Bulgaria's government was in transition; the laws sometimes changed overnight. We showed the agent our passports and he shook his head. Had we come this close only to have to return without our girls?

Then the well-dressed gentleman stepped forward and spoke a few words in Bulgarian. The agent immediately passed us through. Dragging our duffel bags to the Sofia bus, I glanced back at the man whose words had held such power.

After a two-hour ride we arrived in Sofia. The other passengers dispersed, leaving only our bags and us. A driver approached us. 'Taxi?' he asked, quoting an exorbitant fee. What if he tried to charge even more, or steal our valuable cargo? I looked at Stephen. We were both thinking of the twins. *What choice do we have but to get in the taxi?*

Suddenly the man who had assisted us in Plovdiv was at our side, although he had not been with us on the bus. He proceeded to negotiate an honest fare from a couple of taxi drivers. We divided the baggage, and Stephen rode in one cab, our guide and I in another.

'What do you do in Bulgaria?' I finally asked. 'I work with the government,' he said. 'My name is Christos.'

At the hotel our newfound friend wished us well and then walked off into the foggy night. The trials of our trip were over. A few days later we were home with our twins, thanks to our mysterious man in Bulgaria.

STRANGER WITH A FLASK

by Paul DeLisle

A mysterious man appears and saves a sick boy.

The blizzard had raged all day, blanketing the farm with snow and obliterating the roads. Drifts were piled as high as the house. Inside, as night fell, a ten-year-old boy lay in bed, gasping for air. His lungs were weak, the result of having been born prematurely. On that February night in 1933 he had bronchitis and his throat was clogged with phlegm. There was no phone to call a doctor, but even if there had been, none could have made it in this weather. Besides, doctors had given up on the boy's health years ago.

His mother never gave up, though. Ali would say, 'Son, I'm not afraid of you dyin'. I know you'd be safe and happy in heaven. But if it's God's will you live, I'm going to help you all I can.'

The boy had suffered severe colds before and Ali's home remedies always pulled him through. But this time none of her treatments made a difference. His skin had turned a deathly grey-blue. She placed mustard plasters on his chest and under his back. She applied more Vicks to his forehead, smoothing his blond curls. As she listened to the storm howling around their farmhouse and the worsening wheeze in her son's chest, her lips moved in silent prayer. Her husband was nursing his arthritis in the next room. The closest neighbour lived a quarter-mile away. 'What more can I do, Lord?' she asked.

A loud knocking startled her, and she sat quickly upright in her rocker next to the boy's bed. *Who can be out on a night like this?* Ali wondered as she hurried to the kitchen door. A tall man stood on the porch, his coat collar turned up around his face and his hat pulled tightly over his head. In the Depression it wasn't unusual for people down on their luck to stop by and ask for work in exchange for food or a warm place to sleep. 'Come in,' Ali said. 'Make yourself at home.' She gestured to the coffeepot warming on the stove. 'My little boy is sick,' Ali said. 'I need to get back to him.'

But the stranger called after her, 'Wait!' He pointed to a mug on the table. 'Fill it half full of hot water,' he said. Ali, worn out and desperate, snatched up the mug and obediently sloshed water from the kettle into it. 'Bring it here,' he told her. He pulled a flask from his coat and filled the mug with what looked and smelled like whisky. 'Pour this down your son's throat,' he said. 'Get it all into him.'

Ali raced to her boy's room, sat him up and began pouring the near-scalding mixture into his mouth. His face turned fiery red and his eyes opened wide. He grabbed her arm but she tilted his head back and emptied the mug down his throat. The boy gagged, choking and spitting, unable to breathe. Then the hot liquid began to do its work, breaking up the phlegm. Ali held him close to her until he had rid himself of it all. Finally, completely spent, the boy lay down, breathing easily. His skin returned to a healthy pink. 'I have to go thank that man,' Ali said.

But the kitchen was empty. She called to her husband, 'Ed, did you see the man leave?'

The boy's dad appeared in the doorway moving stiffly. 'I never saw him at all,' he said. 'Maybe he's gone out to sleep in the barn.' Ed sat down, painfully pulling on his boots. 'I'll go tell him to come back in.' But Ed found no one in the barn.

The boy listened to his parents in the kitchen as they talked about the stranger. 'I didn't hear Shep bark, did you, Ali?' Ed asked.

'That's why the knock startled me so,' said Ali.

The boy grinned. Their dog went nuts even when a car passed.

'And something else,' Ali said thoughtfully. 'There's no sign he was here. No melted snow, no wet rugs, and no used mug. Ed, when you went out to look for him, the cold air hit me with a blast! I didn't feel any cold air when I let him in.'

That winter night was sixty-three years ago on my family's farm. I was the boy. Some who have heard this story say they knew of the hot whisky remedy, and were surprised my mother didn't think of it. But Ma was dead set against alcohol. She never allowed it in the house, not before and not after that visit. She always welcomed strangers in need, though. That extraordinary night God sent her one who took care of her needs instead, and saved my life.

MUM'S ANGELS

by Jacquelin Gorman

The angels told me that God has chosen my time, but he is allowing me to choose the hour.

'Is there anything in particular you want to talk about?' my mother asked, but with a stranger's voice. I pressed my body deeper into the vinyl-cushioned side of the ambulance. Her throat was so raw from the tubes and machines, and her lungs so saturated with fluid, that even the simplest words were sometimes unintelligible. It was a language I had learned to interpret these last few months. Still, I could not answer her question at first.

My mother smiled patiently. Her face, stripped by cancer to its barest, fragile essence, remained beautiful. With her hairless, smooth head, she appeared at once impossibly old and impossibly young.

'No, Mum, nothing in particular,' I answered. Then I confessed, unable, as always, to lie to her.

'Just everything, Mum. I just want to talk about everything.' *Every big thing and every little thing that will happen to me,* I thought. *I need the answers to all the questions I would have asked you years before, if I had known to ask them. I want your advice on raising my daughter, your first granddaughter, who, now too young to know you, will have to borrow my memories. But most of all let's talk about how I am going to live the rest of my life without you.*

This is what I wanted to say, but I remained silent.

'I know,' she said, in the saddest tone yet of that stranger's voice, as if she had just read my thoughts.

I glanced out of the rear window of the ambulance, stroking the back of Mum's limp hand in a slow, steady rhythm, trying to comfort myself as well as her.

She was breathing so shallowly. I concentrated upon her now tiny body, tiny except for the huge, swollen abdomen, before I detected a slight, uneven movement of her swaddled form. I had nearly stopped breathing myself as I watched her.

I cried out a desperate prayer: *Please, God, wait until we get her home. Let it happen in her own bed, in peace.*

'She has a tumour that is growing rapidly and will result in her death in the next twenty-four hours.' That is what her oncologist had said to us late the night before in the hospital corridor.

My sisters stood with me, flanking our father. I clutched a notepad on which I had carefully written down all our questions. Somehow we had figured that if we just asked this man the right question, he would give us the answer we hoped for. But none of the questions about the quality of our mother's life mattered anymore after being given the answer of death. Still, my father choked one out.

'Will she make it home?' he asked.

The doctor gave my father a look I had seen on his face once before. It was ten months earlier, when the diagnosis had been made, and after listening to his clinical speech my mother had asked him a single question. The room was so quiet, I remember thinking I actually heard the sound of our hearts breaking as she spoke.

'Do I have one good year left?' she had asked.

The doctor had answered my mother then with this same wary expression. It had not even been a year, and certainly not enough of what had occurred since then had been good.

Now my father flinched at the doctor's unspoken message. Then he spoke in a voice I remembered from over twenty years before, an incredibly resonant, strong voice, the way as a child I had imagined God sounded.

'I have arranged for a private ambulance to take my wife home, as soon as she wakes up tomorrow morning. I expect you to be there, and take every tube, and I mean every one, out of her so that she can go home the way she should – the way a person who is as loved and cherished as she is should.'

'Yes, of course,' the doctor said simply. He was visibly relieved. There was nothing else for him to do, and best of all, nothing else he was expected to do. The passing of the torch, so to speak, for the homestretch.

'Have we gone over the bridge yet, darling?' my mother asked, surprisingly alert.

I looked for a familiar landmark and saw that we were slowing down to glide through the sleepy town where my parents had retired a couple of years earlier. I recognized a few of our neighbours outside their houses, standing in a solemn salute.

They had been there for her, the way a rural community knows how to be. Leaving freshly baked casseroles on the doorstep, weeding her flower garden when she was away for chemotherapy, clearing brush from the shoreline so that she could see the water from her bed. People made of solid gold.

'Mum, we're almost there; we're going through town.'

The ambulance crept up our driveway, and I could see my father and sisters standing outside the front door, waiting. Their vigil struck me. So this is how I must look, how we all look, the exposed faces of grief.

How terrible for her to remember us this way. How equally terrible for *us* to remember *her* this way. I threw myself angrily against the doors, just as they opened, and gasped the rain-filled air as I scrambled out.

I have only the foggiest memories of those first hours of my mother's return. I do not remember exact words, or precise events, but at some remarkable point during the early evening, right before our eyes, she turned her own corner, one that no physician had foreseen. And the next morning she woke up, her abdomen completely flat, got out of bed, and made a pot of coffee for her incredulous family.

'There were four angels with me last night,' she announced quietly, her soft voice restored.

My sisters and I smiled at the same time, each of us thinking that she was referring to her four daughters, because angels or not, we had taken turns listening, through the night, from an adjoining room, our ears pressed against a baby monitor, to the sounds of her continued breathing.

'No,' she said, 'four angels came in the night, and each held one corner of the sheet a few inches above my stomach.'

She looked across the table at each of us in succession. My father looked down at his hands.

'And they are waiting for me, but they said that I must have faith because there is still some time left. I know what the doctors have said, but you all must listen to me, because the angels told me. So let's make some plans now.'

Then she proceeded to give us her wish list. To pick up the new boat and go on a family ride across the creek. To have my daughter over to see her one more time. To arrange a small dinner party to thank her closest friends. Small wishes. Yet, the day before, they had been beyond our most far-reaching prayers.

My sisters began a grocery list in preparation for the dinner, and I followed my mother into the bedroom.

'Mum – ' I started to say, not even knowing what my question was.

She adjusted her brightly coloured silk scarf around her bare scalp, and looked up at me defiantly.

'Darling, it was not a dream. It was not even a vision. It happened; *they* were here, as surely as you are standing here right now. And – ' she added, pointing to Danny, our aged golden retriever in his favourite position on the end of her bed, 'he had to shove one of the angels aside last night before he could find a place to lie down. I watched him nudge an angel with his nose so that he could sleep here.'

We both stared at the dog, who rolled his chestnut eyes towards me, tilting his head up proudly, as if he knew full well the importance of being the sole witness to my mother's story.

'So you see, you have time to travel back home and bring my granddaughter here.'

I buried my face in the dog's neck, hiding my bewilderment, and listened blissfully to her plans. I had always believed that if God had to choose one animal to enter heaven, it would be a golden retriever.

'The angels told me that God has chosen my time,' she said, 'but he is allowing me to choose the hour.'

Indeed he did. During the next few weeks she hosted her dinner party, although informally attired in her nightclothes, and she had Communion in her living room, the minister stepping over the sleeping dog so as not to spill the wine. She went out on the water for a short ride on a calm day in my father's new boat. She saw my daughter once more and listened to her giggle the way only a two-year-old, untouched by the closeness of death, can. And more small things, but enormous to us by the mere fact of their occurrence. Each one a gift from God, through her to us.

Six weeks later my mother chose her hour. She was home, sleeping in her bed, holding my father's hand. I am sure God was nearby. And I am surer still that even closer to her side were those friends that only my mother and our dog had been granted the privilege to meet, returning once more to reclaim their precious charge.

2

WHEN LOVE IS
RE-DISCOVERED

Do all the good you can,
By all the means you can,
In all the ways you can,
In all the places you can,
At all the times you can,
Top all the people you can,
As long as you ever can.

John Wesley

THE GREAT EXPERIMENT

by Tom Anderson

A partnership is reinvented on holiday.

I made the vow to myself on the drive down to the beach cottage we'd rented for our holiday on the Jersey Shore. For two weeks I would try to be the loving husband and father Evelyn had always wanted me to be. Totally loving. No ifs, ands or buts about it.

The idea for this drastic experiment had come to me as I listened to the voice of a marriage counsellor on the car's tape player. 'You husbands must be careful of your wives, being thoughtful of their needs,' the voice said. I knew that I had often been a selfish kind of husband, probably much too self-centred, but as a partner in a Wall Street investment firm, I worked hard. So, after all, surely I deserved a bit of coddling?

'Love is an act of will. A person can *choose* to love,' said the voice on the tape. Ashamedly, I had to admit that with Evelyn I often failed to choose love. In petty ways, really. Chiding her for her tardiness; insisting on the TV channel *I* wanted to watch; in my attitude that yesterday's news is worthless, throwing out day-old newspapers that I knew Evelyn still wanted to read. Well, for two weeks all that would change.

And it did. Right from the moment I kissed Evelyn at the door and said, 'That new yellow sweater looks great on you, darling.'

'Oh, Tom, you noticed,' she said, obviously surprised and pleased. Maybe a little perplexed.

After the long drive down, I wanted to sit and read. Evelyn suggested a walk on the beach. I started to refuse, but then I thought; *Evelyn's been alone here with the kids all week and now she wants to be alone with me*. We walked on the beach, while the kids flew their kites.

So it went. Two weeks of not calling the office; a visit to the shell museum, though I usually hate museums; holding my tongue while Evelyn's getting ready made us late for a dinner date with friends. Relaxed and happy; that's how the whole holiday passed, so much so that I made a new vow to keep on remembering what the counsellor had said. Even when we went home again. I would continue to *choose* love.

There was one thing that went wrong with my experiment, however. It's something Evelyn and I laugh about today. On the last night at our cottage, preparing for bed, I saw Evelyn staring at me with the saddest expression.

'What's the matter, honey?' I asked.

'Tom,' she said, sniffling, then looking pleadingly into my eyes. 'Do you know something I don't?'

'What do you mean?'

'Well ... that check-up I had several weeks ago ... our doctor ... did he tell you something about me? Tom, you've been so good to me. Am I dying, Tom?'

It took a minute for it all to sink in. Then I burst out laughing.

'No, love,' I said, wrapping her in my arms, 'you're not dying, but I'm just starting to live!'

THEY NEVER SAID HELLO

by Cecilia Reed

Old Greenhut and his wife were the unfriendliest people I've ever known.

On the block where I grew up, neighbours often met on our front step to laugh and gossip and have a good time – until the Greenhuts showed up. Nothing could put an end to the conversation faster than the arrival of old Greenhut and his wife. This elderly couple lived in the apartment next to us on the ground floor of an old brick building in the city centre. The old man had once worked in a tailor shop in the neighbourhood, but had long since retired He always wore a black, peaked skullcap on his head and a thread-bare overcoat that never quite covered the fringes of his prayer shawl. His wife was small and grey and wore drab-coloured dresses that were long even for the early sixties. When they walked together in the street, she stayed close by his side and kept her eyes riveted to the pavement.

Their routine never varied – every Friday evening and Saturday morning they walked slowly down the few blocks to the little synagogue to attend the Sabbath (Shebbos) services. Otherwise, they remained inside their apartment.

To us neighbourhood kids, they were a regular nuisance. Early on Saturday morning Mr Greenhut would stick his head out the window, which overlooked the shady, tree-lined street, our favourite playground. He could see us playing ball or riding our bikes and he'd call out in a thick Polish accent, 'Go home! You are

49

bad Jewish children! You should be saying your Shebbos prayers and reading the Torah!'

Perhaps the old man wasn't completely wrong – but nevertheless we would taunt back, 'Greenhuts are green nuts!' as we ran or rode down the street as fast as we could. I knew that our behaviour was bad – Dad told me enough times – but I'd ask myself, *Was theirs any better?*

My father was one of the few people who made any effort to even speak to them. He'd always wish them good day when he saw them; they would nod and walk on. I was annoyed at his well-meant attempts. As far as I was concerned, the less contact we had to have with them, the better.

Shortly after my tenth birthday, my family and several guests were seated at our kitchen table. It was the second night of Passover and the table was heaped with the soup, roast beef, gefüllte fish, matzos, fruit compotes and honey cakes my mother had prepared for the Seder. The good food and the warmth of the gathering had put everyone in a fine mood, but Dad looked thoughtful. My mother finally asked him, 'Josef, what's the matter? There's such a big black cloud hanging over your nose, I think we should all get our umbrellas!' Everyone laughed but Dad.

'This evening I ran into the Greenhuts in the hall,' he said quietly. 'I can't help wondering what they're doing tonight. At Passover, at least, we should try to share our blessings with others.' He stood up and walked to the door. I groaned inwardly – I knew where he was headed.

Dad went to their door and knocked. After a minute of waiting, the peephole shutter snapped and the door opened part way. Mrs Greenhut looked up at him. 'What is it?' she asked.

'My wife and I thought you and Mr Greenhut might like to join our Seder. We have so much food and not enough mouths to finish it all.'

'No, we have enough. Good night.' She closed the door.

We could see that Dad was upset when he returned. 'Could it really have hurt them to come over for a little cake and wine?' he asked.

Mum said, 'Oh, give up with them already. Old dogs can't be taught new tricks.' I helped myself to another piece of honey cake, relieved at the outcome.

A few months later, a commotion out in the hall woke me up in the middle of the night. I ran to the door and opened it a crack. Two policemen were carrying Mr Greenhut down the stairs on a stretcher. Mrs Greenhut walked beside them. She was wearing her slippers, and a coat thrown over her shoulders was her only protection against the cold night. She looked like a sleepwalker. I watched them go out the front door to the waiting ambulance, and then stumbled back to bed.

In the morning there was a light knock at our door. I went to it. There stood Mrs Greenhut. I stared at her, and there was a moment of strained silence. It was difficult for her to speak. 'Is your father at home?' she asked finally.

Dad came quickly to the door. 'Well, Mrs Greenhut. Please come in, come in,' he said, and brought her into the living room. He gently urged her to sit down. My father looked at me and said, 'Cecelia, fix Mrs Greenhut a glass of tea now.' She was sobbing and hadn't spoken a word yet. As I fixed the tea I realized that this was the first time I had ever seen her without her husband. She was tiny; the overstuffed sofa nearly swallowed her up. I handed her the tea and after managing a few sips, she looked hesitantly at my father.

'My Sam . . . he died last night. It was a heart attack.' Dad started to express his sympathies, but she continued to speak. 'I need now to make the plans for his funeral. There must be a minyan for him.' This is a number necessary in the Orthodox Jewish religion for conducting public worship – ten males above the age of thirteen. 'We can have a service, but I have no one to ask. I am asking you to help me find ten men for a minyan for my Sam.'

My father patted her hand and said, 'Don't worry, Mrs Greenhut, your Sam will have his minyan.'

It was his day off, but he went out and made the arrangements for her. It was not easy, but eventually he talked enough men in our neighbourhood into being part of the service.

In the weeks that followed, Mrs Greenhut dropped by for tea, sometimes staying for dinner. She even began bringing her folding chair outside to join the other ladies in their daily get-togethers. I came home from school one Friday afternoon, and there was Mrs Greenhut sitting in front of our brick building. She saw me and beckoned me over. 'Cecelia, do you think you could visit with me tonight?' she asked. I wasn't sure if I really wanted to, but I told her I'd ask my mother. Mum thought I should go; I would be doing a 'mitzvah' (a good deed) by spending a little time with her.

I went next door after dinner. She greeted me warmly, but her eyes held a serious expression. We sat down in the living room and she absent-mindedly fingered the lace doily on the armrest.

'It's funny,' she said. 'Tonight is Friday and I'm not in synagogue. I was afraid to walk there alone, the streets are so dark. Now that Sam is gone I will have to find someone to walk with. It's sad sometimes, being such an old lady. You are so young yet, but I think maybe you will understand. Cecelia, I have made mistakes in my life, sad mistakes. Years ago, when Sam and I came to this country we were lucky to be alive.'

As she spoke, I remembered my father saying that they had been the only members of their family in Poland to escape the Nazis. Her parents, her brothers and sisters, all had died. She was completely alone. A small old lady in a big, dark apartment. I thought about Mum and Dad next door waiting for me. I suddenly felt glad I had come.

'We had only each other,' she continued. 'We were afraid of everybody else, and so we kept to ourselves. I know now that we should have trusted God more; we didn't really let him in. Going to synagogue every week gave us great strength, but God didn't mean for us to survive so that we could step away from life. It was a challenge to us to really begin to live again, and we didn't see it. I thank God I still have time left to start, time to come back to life.' She reached up to her neck and unfastened her necklace.

'I want to give you something I have had for fifty years, something I have worn through the good times and the bad.' She removed from her neck the chain on which a six-pointed Star of David was hanging. She pressed it into my hand.

At first I refused to take it. 'I couldn't accept something that means so much to you,' I said. But she insisted.

'The Star of David is the age-old symbol of the faith of our people. When you wear it, Cecelia, remember, sometimes, the old lady who finally learned to love people again.' I took the still-warm bit of gold and thanked her. Before I left I turned to her.

'Mrs Greenhut, next Friday night I would be glad to walk to synagogue with you.'

LOVERS MEETING

by Cindy Goss

An unexpected fright brings new romance.

Cindy: A cold wind was gusting as I pulled into the car park directly below the bank that February morning in 1976. The inky sky had a greenish cast to it, just like the typhoons I had experienced growing up as an 'Air Force brat' in Japan, before Dad retired from the military.

Parking close to the retaining wall of the Kenduskeag Stream that knifes through downtown Bangor, I hurried into the bank. Today I was working the teller window as part of my training as a new-accounts clerk.

After the trauma of my divorce the previous year, it was good to be working again. I had an aptitude for figures, and my employers liked my work. Having survived an unsuccessful marriage, I was now going to concentrate on my career.

But the past wouldn't quite die. Christmas had been painful; I remembered holding my baby daughter beneath the tree at my parents' home, hoping, praying, that my ex-husband would be able to make the trip to see us, but he never came.

I had been at the teller window only about two hours when the bank manager came hurrying over to tell us we'd better get our cars out of the car park. An ice jam had broken upstream and the Kenduskeag was going to flood.

What a nuisance, I thought as I sloshed through the ankle-deep water, leaning into the wind. Several other employees were already driving out of the car park. I was hurrying, but by the time I opened the car door the water was swirling around my knees. I glanced up; the silvery sheet that was pouring over the retaining wall was growing and making a dull roar.

I started the car, but when I put it into gear it died. Agghhh! I tried again. Nothing. Water had drowned the engine.

Reluctantly, I decided I'd have to leave the car, wondering what Dad's reaction would be – his nearly new Ford! I pushed the door handle down. It didn't open. I pushed again, harder, leaning against the door. It wouldn't budge. There was too much pressure from the water pushing against the outside.

Inside, it was up to seat level now and coming in faster. Things began to seem unreal – and frightening. I pushed the button to lower the power windows. Nothing happened. The battery was dead, and the windows couldn't be opened manually!

I panicked, fumbling in the glove compartment for something to smash out the windows. Maps and papers went flying – nothing metal. *Dear God, there's got to be something!* Plunging my hands into the icy water, I felt under the seat. Nothing.

Leaning back, half-submerged in the water, I kicked frantically at the window. It had moved only an inch or so when the car, now half-floating, began to tip forward. I screamed as a wave of icy water swept me into the back seat.

Through the rear window I saw a woman sitting on the roof of a car directly behind me, clutching a purse to her breast. I pounded on the window and screamed, 'Get me out! I'm drowning!' Off to the side I could see people standing on higher ground. 'Tell them I'm in here!' I screamed. She stared at me with blank, shocked eyes. The crowd stood and watched, some with hands in pockets. *Why aren't they doing anything?* I thought. To them it was just a show.

I'm going to die, I thought. I prayed, 'Thank you, Lord, for giving me a good life. I've lived it the best I could. I'm really sorry about the mistakes I've made.' My marriage ... how sad that it hadn't worked out. I thought of my lovely little girl. 'Please take care of her, God,' I prayed. She'd have to grow up without me.

The car was tilting, tilting. I slipped my finger through the small opening I had made in the window. At least part of me was out in the blessed, sweet air. Turning my head towards the ceiling two inches above me, I waited to die.

Hal: I was on my way into Bangor that February day to make a bank deposit for the outdoor sports equipment firm I manage. As I crossed the Penebscot River, I realized it had spilled its banks. Chunks of ice were swirling in the swift current and jamming the shore. I had never seen the river so high, and I had lived in the Bangor area all of my twenty-eight years.

At that time, I was just getting over my divorce. The marriage had died of immaturity – we both had been too young, and over the years we had grown apart. She wanted a career; I wanted to run with my friends. Neither of us could talk to the other.

In the year since the break-up. I had played hard at being a carefree bachelor, but it was a hollow existence. Christmas had been awful. I spent part of the holiday with my two children, and we exchanged gifts. But the happiness of the occasion only underscored the tragedy of what had happened to us as a family. I made my excuses and left to spend the evening with a mate, also divorced, trying to pretend it was 'just another day'.

Now, as I headed down the hill towards the bank. I saw a crowd gathered around what appeared to be a lake with cars bobbing in it. The river was flooding into the bank's car park, and sweeping away the cars with it!

I drove as close as I could and parked. I got out and stood with the crowd. A woman sat perched on the roof of a car about a hundred yards out. *They'll do something,* I thought. There'll be a police launch along.

A man came running out of the bank. 'Hey, officer,' he yelled to a policeman, 'there's a woman in a submerged car! I saw her from the third floor!'

Two construction workers standing nearby, grabbed bricks to break the windows and began wading out. But they turned back. The water was too cold and the current too swift.

'It's no use,' one of the cops said. 'Everybody stay out of the water!'

'It's getting higher and higher,' I protested. 'We've got to do something! She's going to drown out there!'

'Nobody's going in!' the cop snapped.

'The heck with you!' I cried, stripping off my coat and shoes. I couldn't just stand there, a life was at stake.

As I hit the icy water, I thought, *don't think about the cold, just go! If you stop, you won't make it.*

Straining hard against the treacherous current, I approached the submerged vehicle. Its back end was visible just under the surface.

Reaching down I felt for the door handle. Since the car was almost completely flooded, the pressure was equalized and the door opened easily. Hanging on to avoid being swept away, I called, 'Can you hear me? Reach me your arm or leg!'

Cindy: With my face still pressed into the tiny airspace under the roof of the car, I heard someone calling in a muffled voice far away, 'Reach me your arm or leg!' I moved my legs over to the passenger side. A hand went around my calf in a vice-like grip and in one quick movement I was pulled under the water and over the seat. There was a cold, painful pressure. I popped to the surface gasping, my arms around my rescuer's neck. I was alive!

He pushed me up onto the car roof and then climbed up himself, collapsing beside me. Then we crouched in the chill wind, sirens and alarms and shouts rising in a deafening crescendo around us, as our clothes slowly froze to our shivering bodies. A boat was heading towards us . . .

Two hours later we were resting comfortably in the hospital, waiting for our temperatures to get back up to normal. We introduced ourselves and learned that we had both been recently divorced. Dad came with dry clothes for me, but before he took me home Hal and I exchanged numbers. He seemed very nice, and somehow I couldn't forget his sparkly blue eyes . . .

A week or so later after Hal had received several civic awards for heroism, my parents invited him to dinner. We had a marvellous evening. I felt so comfortable around Hal. When he left, Dad said to me, 'Cindy, that boy's in love with you. I can tell!'

I have a strong sense that God directs events, and it was almost as if He had intended us to meet, when the time was right.

Hal: Though we didn't realize it, Cindy and I were just playing at life before we were thrown together so dramatically. Both of us had been dating others casually, trying to find ourselves, trying to find happiness. As for me, I had sworn I'd never marry again.

But I had never met a girl like Cindy. Not only was she beautiful, she was intelligent, had a sense of humour and enjoyed people. She had married too young, as I had, but she hadn't let the divorce make her cynical.

In spite of the things she said, I knew she missed being married. Before long she was visiting my apartment and fixing my dinner. Weekends were spent on outings with the kids, hers and mine.

Cindy: God is so good. He gave Hal and me a second chance at life and happiness. In June 1976. Just four months after the rescue, we were married. I used to think that happiness was always around the corner somewhere – just out of sight – so I was never satisfied with what I had, or the way I was living, or who I was.

Then, one wintry day I was saved from drowning by a courageous young man, and now I'm changed. I don't live in the future anymore – I'm content to live today. I'm learning what the Bible meant when it says, 'So do not worry about tomorrow, it has enough worries of its own.'

A CHANGE OF HEART

by Mary Simmons

How was she going to face the worst day of her life?

The coldness in the pit of my stomach settled into a lump as I slipped into the third-row pew of the country church. With my husband beside me, I welcomed the numbness that seemed to be creeping over my body. The sickening sweetness of the funeral flowers made my head giddy, and I closed my eyes against the blur of summer sun filtering through a narrow stained-glass window.

In a subconscious niche of my mind my sister's voice repeated. 'You shouldn't go. If you ask me, it's downright disrespectful to Mother. Besides, you don't belong there.' Why had I not been able to do as my sister had done and blot out that part of my life with my father?

The familiar refrain of 'What a Friend We Have in Jesus', a song I had loved since childhood, filled my being and offered some comfort.

Childhood. I knew that was what had brought me to this strange church, some sixty miles from where I now lived, for my father's funeral.

I sat, listening, until a feeling of movement in the sanctuary brought me back to reality. Just across the aisle 'the family' was filing into the reserved pews nearest the casket. I knew that the woman my father had deserted his family for more than thirty years ago had had a young son at the time. I forced myself to take a furtive glance. Her son, no doubt, and his family, a wife and three teenagers.

'Dearly beloved,' the minister began, and I felt my husband's arm around my shoulder, 'we have gathered here to pay respect to a husband, a father.' The bitter anger I had become so adept at suppressing towards this woman and her family through the years was already spreading over me when I saw the roses. At the head of the casket emblazoned in gold letters across a wreath of red rosebuds were the words 'Our Pops'.

Suddenly I wanted to turn my wrath on these strangers in the middle row. How dare they claim him as theirs! It infuriated me that her grandchildren would take him as theirs when my own children had never known their grandfather.

I wanted to scream. 'He's not your father. He's mine. You're impostors, all of you!' Bitterness washed over me in waves. I wanted to dash the wreath of roses to the floor and run out to the privacy of our car.

Perhaps if the sympathizing congregation knew that there had been no divorce between my parents and that this woman was only a common-law wife, things might be different.

My sister had been right. I should not have come. I was angry with myself. With my husband for allowing me to come. He should not have agreed so readily when I mentioned attending.

With my heart pounding from the surging anger and resentment, I steeled myself against an outburst. I was a teacher and a writer of children's books. I knew how to practise self-control. I had to manage my emotions now.

I closed my eyes and breathed deeply, giving myself over to the strains of 'In the Garden', until the minister's voice began to lull me like the metronome of my daughter's piano practice. I was a child again, and my father with his broad shoulders and jet-black hair was riding a racing horse across the summer fields of our rolling farm. In another scene I stood proudly beside him while the men of the town vowed that I, his baby girl, was his 'spitting image'.

I thought of the times my father travelled. God knows where. And of the times when he came back home, unwrapping his tapering cigar, whistling a tune and cutting a dance step on the boards of the kitchen floor. My heart swelled with remembered love. But I saw, too, Mother's face pursed with pouting. I could not let her know I loved him so.

Oh, he was a ladies man. Painfully, I relived the bitter arguments ending with my father's usual ultimatum, 'It'll be many moons before you see me again', and leaving us children weeping. Had I not withstood the shame and humiliation of our small town's gossip about my father's escapades? Hadn't my love, even though in secret, and my nightly prayers been constant through the years? I worked at keeping myself removed from this place until the service was over, but I was slipping back.

'You, the family,' the minister was saying. His concern, his condolences were, directed towards them. I could feel the bitter gall rising in me. He was *my* father, not theirs.

For the most part I had not tried to make contact through the years. When my father returned for his mother's funeral, I could sense the uneasiness, the shame of his desertion. Even then I had not wanted to hurt my mother. Hadn't she stood by us children when we needed her?

I remembered a more recent occasion. I was autographing one of my books in the large coastal city where he lived. Something compelled me to search the telephone directory for his number. I called and asked him to meet me. I dared not go to a house where *she* was, and he did not ask me to.

We hugged and then he took out his wallet. With the shaking hands of a man growing old, he drew from it a worn news clipping. I recognized it as a picture of me with the write-up of my first book.

And now he was dead. Our oldest son had taken the telephone message of his death from a stranger – perhaps one of those persons sitting across the aisle from me now. Before I knew it, my husband was guiding me from the church and out into the cemetery to the graveside. I had not intended to go there. Why had I put myself through all of this?

Averting my eyes from 'the family', I succumbed to my husband's urging for me to sit in the back row of metal chairs under the awning. Seated across from me, on the other side of the casket. I noticed several familiar faces – the old druggist from the town where I had grown up, one of my father's cousins, an aunt on my father's side.

As the minister's voice resumed its droning, my eyes caught sight of the wreath again. The red roses with 'Our Pops' had been brought from the church to the graveside. With more force than I thought possible I hated these people who sat in front of me pretending to be broken by grief.

Persons began milling about. The service was over. I turned towards my husband only to find him engaged in a conversation with some gentleman behind him. My resentment grew to include him. Couldn't he see that I wanted to get away from here?

Then someone touched me on the arm – and I was face to face with the woman I had hated all these years.

'You're Mary Mice, aren't you? I recognized you from your picture.'

I am sure my face registered a mixture of feelings. I was not prepared for this soft-spoken person before me. I had expected a cheap, coarse-looking woman. Instead, her silver hair lay in loose curls, and dark linen dress covered a somewhat matronly yet neat figure. Her glistening blue eyes held nothing but love as she said, 'Your father was so proud of you'.

Her son took her by the arm and his wife and children flanked either side, their eyes red from weeping.

Standing there at a loss for words I could see that this 'other woman' was not the brazen home-wrecker I had imagined. I could even see why my father had been attracted to her. I didn't condone what he had done to my mother – what he had done to all of us – but I felt my anger melting away. For the first time since hearing of my father's death, I knew I was going to cry. I swallowed a sob. This little family's suffering was real and heartfelt. They had loved my father deeply. I knew what I had to say.

'I know,' I heard myself getting out the words, 'that all of you loved my father very much.'

Her face creased in a sad smile. She reached out and caught my hand. 'God bless you for coming.'

Groups of persons were moving up to offer words of comfort to my father's new family. I squeezed the warm hand that held mine and then my husband was beside me, guiding me between the grave markers to our car.

Tears poured down my face, not tears of anger and resentment but of relief. I was grateful to my husband for his silence. I needed to deal with the change that had taken place in my heart.

Although the sun was almost down, I felt a warm glow. In a flash I knew what had been holding me back all the time. Church-going person though I was, I had not understood that at the heart of real Christian love lies forgiveness. No longer was the wreath of red roses by the grave a threat to my love for my father or to his for me. Rather it was like a circle of love. Why had I not been able to see that the more love there is in one's heart the wider the circle becomes?

Finally I looked at my husband. 'I'm glad we came,' I said 'Very glad.'

He put his hand over mine and nodded.

'Yes,' was all he said.

SAVING A MARRIAGE

by Arthur Gordon

Is it ever possible to pick up the pieces?

We once had some friends whose marriage was drifting towards the rocks. We knew this because each partner expressed increasing dissatisfaction with the other – complaints that often seemed justified.

Then suddenly the bickering and faultfinding ceased. The marriage took on new warmth and vitality. The change was so astonishing that one day I asked the husband what had happened to them.

'Eight words happened to us,' he said. 'Or, to be more accurate, four.' He told me how one day he and his wife found themselves confessing their mutual dissatisfaction to an old physician who had known them both since childhood. The doctor silently listened to all their recriminations. Finally, he said, 'I can give you a prescription that may help. It's an old saying that goes like this: We like someone *because,* we love someone *although*. Think about it carefully. If you can grasp that distinction and make up your minds to apply those last four words to your problems, I think your marriage can be saved.'

It wasn't easy, the husband told me, but they did it. First they prayed about their effort and asked for God's help. Then they stopped expecting or demanding perfection from each other. Each partner decided – it was an act of will, really – to go on loving *although*. And gradually the broken pieces of the marriage came together again.

Might there not be a challenge here for any marriage or any family? Suppose, choosing a quiet moment, one person went to another and said, 'I really love you. I love you *although* sometimes you do this one particular thing that upsets me.'

Wouldn't a lot of smouldering grievances be exposed and resolved? Wouldn't family or marriage ties grow closer? It might take some courage, but if people occasionally told one another that they liked them *because* and loved them *although*, wouldn't that be a healing and strengthening thing?

I think so.

LIFE BEGINS AT 70

by Marjorie and George Holmes

Can you ever find true love a second time around?

Marjorie: On the evening of 1 January 1981, I sat at my desk, anticipating the new year ahead. It had been thirteen months since my husband, Lynn, died. We'd been married forty-seven years and I'd missed him and mourned him. But he'd been desperately sick with cancer and neither our four children nor I had wanted his torment extended by even a single day.

Now, after a year, I felt at peace about Lynn – and myself. God had blessed me with wonderful health. At the age of seventy, I still swam, danced and water-skied. I still had many things to write. And I had even begun to wonder if there might not be another person to share this good life with. *In the New Year,* I thought, *perhaps . . .*

George: On the evening of 1 January 1981, I sat in the bedroom my late wife, Carolyn, and I had shared. I was alone and bitter. In the months since her death, I had been withdrawn, in retreat from my three children and my friends, losing weight, dying inside myself. Carolyn and I had had forty-eight beautiful, ardent years, but now marriage and ardour were lost to me forever. I was too broken; it was too late.

Marjorie: During the year just ended, even my children had encouraged me to think about finding companionship. 'Pray for someone special,' my daughter Melanie had advised. Why not? Lately, each morning after my shower and each night at bedtime,

I'd begun to pray, 'Please, God, send me a wonderful man who will love me and whom I can love.'

I wasn't in any hurry; I just felt if this were God's will, it would happen. Now I took a sheet of paper from my desk drawer and, half-whimsically, I wrote down the qualifications I would desire in a potential husband:

1. A believer, devout.
2. Good health.
3. Successful professionally.
4. Intelligent, well read.
5. Good talker, good listener.
6. Sexy, ardent.
7. Good dancer. (Not absolutely essential, but why not ask for what you want?)

George: When Carolyn died, very suddenly, my whole world collapsed. I was like a child turned out in a strange city in the dark. I didn't know what to do. Carolyn had been my sweetheart and companion but also secretary, bookkeeper and nurse for my medical practice. She handled everything. I never wrote a cheque or paid a bill. I didn't even answer the telephone.

From the day of her death, I was like a zombie, a man literally ill, almost autistic, with grief. To keep my sanity I continued to see patients, but my zest for life was completely gone. I wouldn't even accept a dinner invitation from friends, let alone consider marrying again. It was unthinkable.

Now, sitting in our bedroom on New Year's night, I heard my voice cursing God.

Marjorie: The new year was six weeks old when my phone rang on a bright February morning and I heard a stranger's voice saying, 'I love you. You saved my life'.

I listened. As a writer you learn to listen, sometimes puzzled, always expectant, never shocked. You learn to recognize those whose need is real. This was no crank. The voice, as it went on, told me he was a doctor who had been absolutely devastated by the loss of his wife. Though his family, friends and patients had tried desperately, he'd been inconsolable – lonely, wild with grief, suicidal. Then, on New Year's night he'd come across my book, *I've Got to Talk to Somebody, God,* under quite amazing circumstances.

George: Exactly at the moment I cursed God, a picture of me that had been on Carolyn's dresser pitched forward and crashed to the floor. No wind, no bolt of lightning, just an abrupt crash. Shaken, I dropped to my knees. 'God, forgive me. But help me, *help* me.'

I raised my head and found myself staring at the door of a closet beside the bed, noticing for the first time that its panels formed a cross. Something urged me to open the door and to reach right down under a pile of Carolyn's things – dresses, purses, knitting materials, what have you. And what my fingers found and brought out was, of all improbable things, a book -- a book called *I've Got to Talk to Somebody, God* by Marjorie Holmes.

Reading it helped. It told me that the author had suffered, that a lot of people suffer, but with the help of God they can and must go on. I read it over and over again. I knew that somehow, if only to please my worried family, I had to try to come out of my personal tomb. Finally, I decided to accept the invitation of a Florida couple that had been very close to Carolyn and me. They'd been begging me to visit and on the drive south I could visit my son Jeff.

When I got to where Jeff lives, I opened my suitcase and there on top of my clothes was *I've Got to Talk to Somebody, God.* I didn't even remember packing it! Staring at it, I read the information on the jacket for the first time. The author lived not far away. I had never before as much as written to an author, let alone tried to contact one in person. But now I knew I *had* to try to contact this one, this Marjorie Holmes.

Hours and innumerable phone calls later, I got through to a pleasant man who said, 'Why, yes, her husband was my cousin – he died about a year ago. Yes, I'll give you her number.'

Marjorie: The man on the phone went on to tell me that after God had put my book in his hands, it had literally pursued him on this trip. He felt he had to call me.

'Somehow, I knew you'd been widowed before I heard about it,' he added. 'If you're still free, may I come to see you?'

'Yes, I'm free,' I said, pleased and touched. 'But unfortunately I'm just leaving on a two-week speaking trip.'

'I'll stay on with my son till you come back,' he insisted. And, unlikely as it seemed at the time, he did.

When I returned I called, simply because I'd promised, and he whooped for joy. 'Will you have dinner with me tomorrow night?'

The next evening a handsome six-foot man walked in the door, his arms full of roses. On the way to the restaurant he sang to me in the most beautiful male voice I've ever heard. He was poised and gallant and funny and for real. He had brought along his little black doctor's bag full of pictures, clippings and credentials.

We talked for hours. And when he kissed me it seemed perfectly in order. But when he asked me to marry him, I said no, firmly but gently. 'Not because this is so sudden. Because you're still in love with your wife, George. And from all the things you've told me, I know I never could be the kind of wife she was to you.'

George: Mere weeks ago, I'd found the idea of remarrying unthinkable. Now I was begging for the hand of a woman I'd met in person only a few hours earlier. And I'd never felt surer of myself in my life.

'But I love *you* now!' I told Marjorie when she rejected my proposal. 'The past is gone, it's all over. Something happened the minute I heard your voice. It was like waking up from a nightmare. And when I actually saw you, it's not your book, it's you, the wonderful time we've had together just in these past few hours. We need each other. God himself must have brought us together. Please say you'll at least make an effort to get to know me?'

Patiently she explained just how difficult that would be. 'You're practicing, and I'm researching a new book and still winding up promotion commitments on the last one. I'm really not right for you, George. A large part of me will always be married to my career.'

'But at least you'll let me drive over to see you again?'

'I'm sorry. I'm packing for a trip to Israel. Maybe when I get back.'

I took her home docilely, but I didn't take no for an answer. Marjorie relented and let me visit – and see her off for Israel. When she came back, three weeks later, I was waiting at the airport with an armload of flowers. I bombarded her with letters, phone calls, gifts and more flowers. Then I persuaded her to spend the week before Easter with me, visiting my son Jeff.

It was a marvellous, carefree week of running the dogs on the beach, swimming, dancing. Never had I enjoyed anyone's company so much. And the most wonderful part: Marjorie seemed to take an equal pleasure in *me*. On Easter Sunday, as we knelt together in church, I worked up the courage to try again. Squeezing her hand, I asked the crucial question.

Marjorie: 'Yes, oh, yes!' I whispered. Never mind that here was a man who would never get over his wife (I thought). Never mind that I couldn't balance a chequebook, let alone fill the multiple roles that Carolyn had filled for him. What really mattered was that God *had* sent me 'a wonderful man who loved me and whom I could love.' And did!

We rushed home from church and called our families. They were thrilled. Eventually we chose 4 July for our wedding day and planned an outdoor summer ceremony. It rained torrents that day. But the sun broke through just an hour before the appointed time. People mopped off the chairs, the minister arrived, and the music began to play. I wore a pink dress, the colour of the sunset. And as George and I joined hands to repeat our vows, the most beautiful rainbow I have ever seen arched the sky.

When we returned from our honeymoon and I was packing up books and papers for the move to George's home, I came across the forgotten list of qualifications I'd written for my future husband. 'George, you won't believe this,' I told him, and read them aloud.

'Who is this guy?' he grinned. Then, taking the list to look for himself, he exclaimed. 'You mean you wrote this on January the first?'

I nodded.

'About what time?'

'Around ten at night, as I recall. Why do you ask?'

'That's when it happened! When the picture fell! When I was in such terrible despair until something told me to reach into the closet and I found your book!'

The picture falling. The book turning up in his closet and later in his suitcase. His son living in the vicinity of my home. His tracing a number that proved to be that of Lynn's cousin. I remember reading somewhere 'There are no coincidences, only God incidences'.

George: Since our marriage, I've continued to see patients and Marjorie has continued to write. We're both convinced that the best way to live a vital, enthusiastic life is to keep doing the work that satisfies you. As for love, I think it's like a savings account. It draws interest and builds. If your first marriage was rich in love, that means you have an even greater store of love to lavish on the second.

Marjorie: I agree with George about love generating more love. Even so, I must try to answer an important question. Is it possible to take the place of a mate who has been loved so long?

No. That place will be separate and sacred forever. What the second husband or wife must realize is that a *new* place has been created. And the second love is no less thrilling, beautiful and enduring simply because this new door to the heart has been opened later.

As George says, the richer and finer the love that has gone before, the greater this second love can be.

And truly, our life together grows sweeter with every year.

A CHRISTMAS CRISIS

by Melva Smith

A young woman breaks through the pain of isolation.

I stared out the window at the snow as big flakes covered the two narrow front steps. Always before, I had thrilled at December snowfalls, the perfect backdrop to the carols Dad and I sang as we hung lights on the two spruce trees flanking our door. But not this year. And not that front door. This was the first Christmas since Dad had asked Mum for a divorce.

Mum had taken a small house and moved out, leaving Dad in our old house. She was always the one to be decisive, always at the helm. She had taken a job when we four kids reached college age and turned each pay cheque over to whichever college we attended; she'd hunted jumble and car boot sales to clothe us, and stretched chicken casseroles to feed Dad's business associates and our own friends.

Now she was alone, except for me. I, the youngest, had just finished college and was job hunting. In the six months she'd lived in the cramped cracker-box house on this narrow street with one tree per yard, she'd forged ahead with her life. She'd returned to school to complete her degree, taken a part-time job and joined a support group of divorced women.

But now as Christmas approached, something had changed in her. I'd often find her sitting in the dark, just sitting, staring. Sometimes I'd go to her and sit beside her, and she'd reach for my hand and turn to me and say, 'I'm bitter, Melva. I think about Dad with that other woman, and I'm hurt and angry and oh so … lonely.'

I too was angry. I never thought I could hate my dad, but I did now. I hated him for what he had done to us. Now with Christmas coming, it all seemed too much. 'Mum, why don't we just forget about Christmas this year?' I asked.

'No, we can't do that,' she said. 'We'll have Christmas here. I'll invite everybody here – all you children, I mean.'

'How?' I asked. 'There's not enough room! We can't even open out the dining room table and fit the chairs underneath!'

'We'll just have to eat Christmas dinner off our laps.'

'And there'll be Dad rattling around in that big house. I hope he starves! You know he can't boil an egg,' I retorted hotly.

We spent the next two weeks like zombies, going through the motions of preparing for a celebration. Each task filled me with more anger. Our tiny tree reminded me of the roomy house I'd lost; one fewer gift to buy symbolized a family unit that existed no more. The same songs and scents that brought pleasure for years now underscored how everything had changed.

On Christmas Eve I dashed into a department store to make a last-minute purchase. I elbowed my way towards a table to find the perfect pair of maroon gloves, but my mind wasn't on the purchase, it was on how angry I felt. My two older sisters had jobs; my brother was married and had a child. They had separate lives. Mum was suffering. And Dad – well, he had removed himself from us.

Now I stood stock still in the middle of the hat-and-glove department while carols rang out over the store's loudspeakers. Christmas was coming and I didn't want to be a part of it. I had never felt lonelier in my life.

When I got home, Mum was humming. She was actually cheerful. The refrigerator was stocked with food for the next day. There was Mum's cranberry mould and celery and carrot spike soaking in water. Black olives were chilled, the turkey was thawing, and the sage and onion stuffing was piled high in a bowl covered with plastic wrap.

'Here, Mel,' Mum said, using my childhood nickname and handing me an apron, 'help me with the Christmas cake.'

Had something in her spirit changed, or was she just doing a better job of covering up? Not wanting to spoil the moment, I accepted the apron. We cut out the familiar forms of angels, bells, stars and reindeer, and even joined in snatches of carols. The cake was in the oven when my brother arrived with his wife and their small son, Joey. We had supper and it was time to leave for the Christmas Eve service. Time was not standing still. Christmas was upon us, ready or not.

The next morning I awoke to the familiar aromas of the Christmas turkey roasting, and of fresh coffee and cinnamon buns, which were Mum's Christmas breakfast treat. My two older sisters arrived midmorning with packages and suitcases. Mother and I would sleep in the basement and give them our twin beds.

The living room soon became a circus with my nephew, Joey, flinging himself upon his packages, and with our own glee at surprise gifts from one another. I think we all overdid it in an effort to pretend nothing had changed.

We were at the stage of saving bows and collecting up tissue paper when the doorbell rang. Mum opened the door and there stood Dad.

The room went silent as we gaped at him. 'Come in, Richard,' Mum said. Dad entered the room, looking about tentatively, assessing his welcome. I couldn't believe it. Had Mum invited him here? How could she have? How *could* she?

Joey sailed through this startling moment by tackling Dad's knees. 'Hi, Grandpa!'

I turned and fled into the kitchen. I was pretending to check on the turkey a few minutes later when Mum came in and put a hand on my shoulder. I confronted her at once.

'Why?' I demanded.

'Melva,' she started, 'I wasn't sure that Dad was coming or I would have told you ahead of time.'

Quietly she took my hand. 'Last night, didn't we pray, "Forgive us . . . as we forgive those who have sinned against us"?'

'Mum,' I said trembling, 'I *can't*.'

'What's the alternative?' she asked, her voice stronger. 'Didn't you see how you and I have been living this month? If we let anger and hurt cut us off, we're isolating ourselves. Then something you said stuck in my head. About Dad rattling about in that big house alone, and how you hoped he starved. I knew we didn't want spiteful thoughts in our heads, especially at Christmas. I wondered if we couldn't set them aside for one day. So I called him.'

'But Mum, he could have hung up on you or said hurtful things!'

'I know. That's the chance I took. I had to set aside my pride to do it. I knew I was taking a risk, but I counted on God's Spirit – his *Christmas* Spirit. And that's what I'm counting on to carry us through the day.'

'After the way he's treated you – treated us all!'

'Listen,' she said firmly, 'we had some good years, your dad and I. To me, you kids are permanent good that came out of those years. There's a lot of life still ahead of us – weddings, graduations, birthdays. I don't want you to have to ask, "Shall we invite Mother to this, or Dad?" That would separate us all even further. No, Melva, I am going to love your father and you are going to love him, and no matter what the cost to our pride and vanity, we are going to do it.'

She put her arm around me and we went back out.

After we sat down to Christmas dinner, things got easier. As the afternoon passed, Dad even dozed on the sofa while my sisters and I modelled our gifts, and we all tried on a red-brimmed hat, giggling as always. It was tempting to pretend nothing had changed, and painful to remember things had.

I lay on my bed that night and stared into the darkness of the basement, listening to the water pipes and the hum of the furnace. We had made it through Christmas day. Looking back, I'd spent far more energy dreading it than living it.

Future Christmases would be easier now, thanks to Mum. And the feeling of loneliness had gone. With Mum too. Love had pushed out the anger inside us.

PRODIGAL FATHER

by Dale Kugler

An old ironworker learns that he is loved.

At seventy-three, Marcia Pollock's father was a man of great independence, a man of great pride. He had been an ironworker, a career that gave him great satisfaction, even looking back. He loved to point out to his grandchildren the construction jobs he had worked on, the huge advertising structures in and around town. The kids called him 'Poppy', a contagious name that everybody used.

Poppy lived in a furnished room in his old neighbourhood and he had a part-time job at a local pharmacy. After Marcia's mother died, Poppy had firmly and flatly refused Marcia and Jack's invitation to come and live with them. He was stubborn about not intruding on their lives, about not crowding their little house, about not becoming a burden.

Yet the truth of the matter was that they really wanted him. Poppy was good to be around. He was always on the up side, always helpful. The kids loved him because he listened to them and worked with them and because he always brought them something. There were always special gifts on birthdays and at Christmas. And whether it was a little bunch of flowers for Marcia, or a new after-shave for Jack, Poppy simply never arrived empty-handed.

And so it was with shock and bewilderment that Marcia went to see Poppy in the hospital that summer after he had collapsed in the street. The doctors told Marcia, Poppy had been living on coffee and doughnuts.

'Why, Poppy, why?' Marcia wanted to know. 'There's no reason to go without food. You have money. You have us.'

But Poppy just brushed the whole subject aside.

'You're wrong,' the pharmacist told Marcia later that day. 'He has practically no money at all – just the government cheque and what little he makes here. Yet I myself saw him spend most of his last cheque on your little boy's bicycle.'

She became stern with Poppy. 'You're foolish, Poppy,' she said.

'I have my pride,' Poppy answered.

'False pride,' she hurled back at him.

During autumn, Poppy didn't come around as often as he had in the past, but when he did, he would still arrive with little gifts in hand, and he would look at Marcia with a defiance she had never seen in him.

'I can't come over Christmas Day,' Poppy told her just before the holidays. 'This year I promised I'd watch the store.'

Marcia knew the shop was not open on Christmas.

From then on she grew more distressed with each day that passed. She had to do something, but she floundered until the morning she sat down and wrote the letter.

Poppy dear –

This will be brief. We'll miss you at Christmas, all of us, because you are one of us. I am praying for you – as always.

And, Poppy, lately I've been thinking about the parable of the prodigal son and it's meaning, especially in the confusion of Christmas. What's more important in that situation, the destruction of pride – or the triumph of love?

We love you.

Marcia

All Christmas morning Marcia thought about Poppy. Half an hour before the turkey went on the table, the doorbell rang. Marcia jumped. She knew it was Poppy.

The kids rushed to him and in their great surprise inundated Poppy with more hugs and kisses than he had ever had before. Poppy then looked at Marcia. Now there was no defiance in his eyes, only snap and sparkle like the Poppy of old. Yet there was something else, a look of triumph, the look of a battle won.

Poppy held out his arms to Marcia, and his hands, those strong ironworker's hands, were empty, utterly empty – yet never had they been more filled.

A GOLDEN MARRIAGE

by Faye Field

I've heard others say that financial insecurity makes for trouble in marriage, but Tommy and I started out poor.

Tommy was a football coach, I was a book lover. Tommy was an only child, accustomed to the calm of a small household. I grew up with one brother and four sisters, all of us used to talking at once. Tommy has always been practical, even-tempered, and pragmatic. I am sensitive, easily hurt, and too quick to respond to praise. When Tommy and I were married, many wondered how we would get along. That was fifty years ago.

Sometimes I wonder if we have stayed married that long because I learned to put down a Shakespeare play for the thrill of seeing Tommy's boys play. Or because he learned to look into the books I discussed at dinner. Maybe it's because I came to depend upon his equable temperament to calm me down. Or, that he came to love all the hugging and exclaiming that took place at our Bunch family reunions.

No, I suppose a couple doesn't need to be exactly alike to stay together.

I've heard others say that financial insecurity makes for trouble in marriage, but Tommy and I started out poor. We were both teachers at Weatherford College, and on his meagre salary, Tommy had to borrow money to buy my wedding ring.

And what about those unexpected discoveries you make in each other? I found out that casseroles are not the way to a man's heart –

yet I also learned that a husband can still love his wife even when he hates some of her cooking. Tommy discovered that it takes a man less time to dress than it does a woman – but that it might be worth the wait. We both had to see that friendly conversation with the opposite sex does not necessarily mean flirtation.

They say that being together, never separating, is essential for a strong union, but in our first years of marriage, World War II took Tommy away in the Navy. For many long months we could communicate only by letter, yet somehow, even then, Tommy and I were close.

Yes, I know a couple should always work on their faults. But alas, after fifty years of trying, I still fail to dust the top of the fridge and Tommy still forgets to close the bathroom door. Some things we've learned to overlook. Tommy says nothing about the lists I constantly compile. And when he says he is in no hurry and yet waits for me in the car with the engine running, I'm no longer irked. Maybe that's because when I ask him to forgive me, he always says, 'There's nothing to forgive; I've already forgotten it.'

I'm sure the little niceties have helped smooth our years together. Tommy never leaves the dining table without thanking me for the meal I've cooked. And I tell him he is as handsome as ever, which is true. I still can't believe I won over all those girls who were after this good-looking football hero. I am like David: 'Blessed be the Lord God of Israel which sent thee this day to meet me.'

But after fifty years of marriage, what do I have to say to a new bride and groom? I think of something my father told a young man who was just starting out in farming: 'I've worked in the fields a long time,' said Dad, 'and I'll tell you what you need. Love the land, don't mind hard work, and trust in the Lord for things you can't control, like rain, wind, sunshine and storms.'

My advice? Love your spouse, work hard, and trust in the Lord in rain and shine. That ought to be about it.

3

WHEN HEAVEN IS
AT HAND

The door of death is made of Gold,
That mortal eyes cannot behold:
But when the mortal eyes are closed,
And cold and pale the limbs reposed,
The soul awakes, and wondering sees
In her mild hand the golden keys

William Blake

RETURN FROM TOMORROW

by Dr George Ritchie

A young army private experiences an astonishing new world that changes his life forever.

When I was sent to the base hospital at Camp Barkeley, early in December 1943, I had no idea I was seriously ill. I'd just completed basic training, and my only thought was to get on the train that would take me to medical school as part of the Army's doctor-training programme. It was an unheard of break for a private, and I wasn't going to let a chest cold cheat me out of it.

But days passed and I didn't get better. It was 19 December before I was moved to the recuperation wing, where a jeep was to pick me up at 4 o'clock the following morning to drive me to the station.

A few more hours and I'd make it! Then about 9.00 p.m. I began to run a fever. I went to the sister and begged some aspirin. Despite the painkiller, my head throbbed, and I'd cough into the pillow to smother the sounds. At 3.00 a.m. I decided to get up and dress.

The next half-hour is a blur for me. I remember being too weak to finish dressing. I remember a nurse coming to the room, and then a doctor, and then a bell-clanging ambulance ride to the X-ray building. Could I stand, the captain was asking, long enough to get one picture? I struggled unsteadily to my feet. The whir of the machine is the last thing I remember.

When I opened my eyes, I was lying in a little room I had never seen before. A tiny light burned in a nearby lamp. For a while I lay

83

there, trying to recall where I was. All of a sudden I sat bolt upright. The train! I'd miss the train!

Now, I know that what I am about to describe will sound incredible. I do not understand it any more than I ask you to; all I can do is relate the events of that night as they occurred. I sprang out of bed and looked around the room for my uniform. Then I stopped, staring. Someone was lying in the bed I had just left.

I stepped closer in the dim light, and then drew back. He was dead. The slack jaw, the grey skin was awful. Then I saw the ring. On his left hand was the ring I had worn for two years. I ran into the hall, eager to escape the mystery of that room. Medical school, that was the all-important thing – just getting there. I walked down the hall towards the outside door.

'Look out!' I shouted to a nurse bearing down on me. She seemed not to hear, and a second later had passed the very spot where I stood as though I had not been there.

It was too strange to think about. I reached the door, went through and found myself in the darkness outside, speeding towards the station. Running? Flying? I only know that the dark earth was slipping past while other thoughts occupied my mind, terrifying and unaccountable ones. The nurse had not seen me. What if the people at medical school could not see me either?

In utter confusion I stopped by a call box in a town by a large river and put my hand against the telephone. At least the phone *seemed* to be there, but my hand could not make contact with it. One thing was clear: In some unimaginable way I had lost my firmness of flesh, the hand that could grip that phone, the body that other people saw.

I was beginning to know too that the body on that bed was mine, unaccountably separated from me, and that my job was to get back and rejoin it as fast as I could.

Finding the base and the hospital again was no problem. Indeed, I seemed to be back there almost as soon as I thought of it. But where was the little room I had left? So began what must have been one of the strangest searches ever to take place – the search for myself. As I ran from one ward to the next, past room after room of sleeping soldiers, all about my age, I realized how unfamiliar we are with our own faces. Several times I stopped by a sleeping figure that was exactly as I imagined myself. But the ring was lacking, and I would speed on.

At last I entered a little room with a single dim light. A sheet had been drawn over the figure on the bed, but the arms lay along the blanket. On the left hand was the ring. I tried to draw back the sheet, but I could not grip it. And now that I had found myself, how could one join two people who were so completely separate? And there, standing before this problem, I thought suddenly, *This is death. This is what we human beings call 'death', this splitting up of one's self.* It was the first time I had connected death with what had happened to me.

In that most despairing moment, the little room began to fill with light. I say 'light', but there is no word in our language to describe brilliance that intense. I must try to find words, however, because incomprehensible as the experience was to my intellect, it has affected every moment of my life since then.

The light, which entered that room, was from heaven. I knew because a thought was put deep within me: *You are in the presence of God.* I have called him 'light', but I could also have said 'love', for that room was flooded, pierced, illuminated, by total compassion. It was a presence so comforting, so joyous and all-satisfying that I wanted to lose myself forever in the wonder of it.

But something else was present in that room. There also entered every single episode of my entire life. There they were, every event and thought and conversation, as palpable as a series of pictures. There was no first or last, each one was contemporary. Each one asked a single question, *What did you do with your time on earth?*

I looked anxiously among the scenes before me: school, home, scouting and the cross-country team – a fairly typical boyhood, yet in the light of that presence it seemed a trivial and irrelevant existence.

I searched my mind for good deeds. *Did you tell anyone about me?* came the question.

'I didn't have time to do much,' I answered. 'I was planning to, and then this happened. I'm too young to die.'

No one, the thought was inexpressibly gentle, is too young to die. And now a new wave of light spread through the room, already so incredibly bright, and suddenly we were in another world. Or rather, I suddenly perceived all around us a very different world occupying the same space. I followed through ordinary streets and countryside's, and everywhere I saw this other existence strangely superimposed on our familiar world.

It was thronged with people. People with the unhappiest faces I have ever seen. Each grief seemed different. I saw businessmen walking the corridors of the places where they had worked, trying vainly to get someone to listen to them. I saw a mother following a sixty-year-old man, her son, I guessed, cautioning him, instructing him. He did not seem to be listening.

Suddenly I was remembering myself, that very night, caring about nothing but getting to medical school. Was it the same for these people? Had their hearts and minds been all concerned with earthly things, and now, having lost earth, were they still fixed hopelessly here? I wondered if this was hell: to care most when you are most powerless.

I was permitted to look at two more worlds that night. I cannot say 'spirit worlds', for they were too real, too solid. Both were introduced the same way a new quality of light, a new openness of vision, and suddenly it was apparent what had been there all along. The second world, like the first, occupied this very surface of the earth, but it was a vastly different realm. Here was no absorption with earthly things, but – for want of a better word – with truth.

I saw sculptors and philosophers here, composers and inventors. There were universities and great libraries and scientific laboratories that surpass the wildest inventions of science fiction.

Of the final world I had only a glimpse. Now we no longer seemed to be on earth, but immensely far away, out of all relation to it, and there, still at a great distance, I saw a city – a city, if such a thing is conceivable, constructed out of light. At that time I had not read anything on the subject of life after death. But here was a city in which the walls, houses, streets seemed to give off light, while moving among them were beings as blindingly bright as the One who stood beside me. This was only a moment's vision, for the next instant the walls again closed around me, the dazzling light faded, and a strange sleep stole over me.

To this day, I cannot fully fathom why I was chosen to return to life. All I know is that when I woke up in the hospital bed in that little room, in the familiar world where I'd spent all my life, it was not a homecoming. The cry in my heart that moment has been the cry of my life since: to see that world again.

It was weeks before I was well enough to leave the hospital, and all that time one thought obsessed me: to get a look at my chart. At last I was left unattended. There it was in terse medical shorthand: Pvt. George Ritchie, died 20 December 1943, double lobar pneumonia.

Later I talked to the doctor who had signed the report. He told me there was no doubt in his mind that I was dead when he examined me, but nine minutes later the soldier who had been assigned to prepare me for the morgue came running to him to ask him for a shot of adrenalin. The doctor gave me a hypo of adrenalin directly into the heart muscle, all the while disbelieving what his own eyes were seeing. My return to life, he told me, without brain damage or other lasting effect, was the most baffling circumstance of his career.

Today I feel that I know why I had the chance to return to this life. It was to become a physician so that I could learn about man and then serve God. And every time I have been able to serve by helping some broken-hearted adult, treating some injured child or counselling some teenager, then deep within I have felt that he was there beside me again.

THE AWAKENING

by Michelle Yates

Strange music in the night brings comfort to a saddened family.

During the early morning hours of a warm night in June 1987, I was asleep in our home when something caused me to awaken. At first I thought I was dreaming. But no, I was sure I was awake, and still I heard it. Music. Beautiful, melodic strumming. I got up to check if someone had left a radio or TV on, but that wasn't it. I looked in on our four children to see if any of them was up playing a record. But all were sound asleep – except for our two-year-old, Jez, who was staring out of the window.

'Jez, what are you doing?'

He turned towards me, his blue eyes wide. 'Mummy, I hear songs.'

I crouched down by his curly blond head and looked out of the window, but I saw nothing, just the leaves on the tree. I picked him up. 'Sweetheart, I hear it too. But let's try to go back to sleep.' As I carried him back to bed and plumped up his Donald Duck pillow, my heart pounded. What *was* it?

Back in our bedroom I woke my husband, Michael. 'Do you hear the music?' I asked. Groggily he shook his head and was soon snoring again.

The beautiful strumming became louder. Then it stopped, and a lovely high-pitched voice began to sing, coming from the direction of our fenced-in, aboveground, swimming pool. I clearly heard the words:

In all things give Him praise.
In all your days give Him your praise.
He alone is worthy of your praise.
Though you be racked with pain,
Still proclaim He is Lord
And give Him praise. . .

Next morning, as bright sunshine filled the house, and Mike went off to his job as an electronics engineer at the Highland Park Chrysler plant, I wondered if it had been a dream. Then as I poured cornflakes, Jez asked, 'Mummy, who was that singing last night?'

I caught my breath, my mind whirling. Jez was soon rolling his little car across the breakfast table, but I continued to wonder. The message had sounded like what I'd always thought the singing of angels would be, and I've always believed in angels, God's messengers. But if it was indeed the music of angels, what could it mean? Jez and I were the only ones, apparently, who had heard anything. I just didn't know what to make of the strange experience.

Two months later, on Wednesday, 19 August 1987, Jez was so wound up that he didn't want to nap. Always a climber, he was up on the sofa back then on my kitchen counters. Finally he crawled next to me on my bed, laid his head on my chest, and then looked up. 'Game, Mummy.'

It was a little amusement we enjoyed. I pointed to his eye and said, 'Eye, eye,' then to his nose, 'nose, nose,' and on to his mouth, teeth and cheek. I brushed my fingers through his soft blond curls and he laughed. Then, as always, I ended by saying, 'Mummy loves you, Jez.'

He kissed me and said, 'Jez loves you too.' He relaxed and, looking at the picture over my bed, whispered, 'Mummy, that's Jesus.' I was thrilled. I had been trying to teach him that for months.

At supper Jez was the clown as usual. He had learned a new giggle, and all of us had fun in our attempts to mimic him. Afterwards, the children asked to go swimming. I wasn't feeling well, so Mike said he would watch them while I rested on the sofa. Soon I dozed off.

Suddenly I was wakened. 'Mummy, Jez fell in the pool!' It was six-year-old Athena, her eyes wide in terror.

I leapt up and raced out the back door. There on the pools wooden deck Jez lay wet and motionless. Mike was bending over him, frantically giving him CPR. 'Call the police!' Mike yelled.

In minutes, Mike and our landlord, who lives nearby, were putting Jez into our van to rush him to hospital. Before leaving, Mike brokenly explained that while he was in the basement getting some toys, he hadn't noticed that Jez had slipped out of the house and climbed the pool fence.

Athena, five-year-old Gabriel and three-year-old Josiah were crying. 'Jez is dead!' screamed Athena. 'I don't want my baby brother to be dead!'

'We don't know that,' I soothed. Then I sat them down. 'Look, Jez is in the hands of God. We must trust him. Now let's pray for Jez to be strong. We are a family, and must stay together no matter what.'

I put our children in the care of neighbours and rushed to the hospital. There Mike and I waited, gripping each other's hands.

When the doctor appeared, her face was grave. 'We finally got a faint heartbeat,' she said. 'But,' she touched my shoulder, 'you must remember, there may be some brain damage.'

'I don't care,' I cried. 'I just want my baby back alive.'

Finally, they let us see Jez. He was lying in the trauma room with machines beeping. I brushed wet curls from his closed eyes. How small and helpless he looked. Soon a helicopter came to whisk him to a special hospital that the doctor said was the best paediatric centre in the area.

Mike went home for Jez's Donald Duck pillow and his favourite shirt and pants for him to wear when he came home. When we waited at the hospital I felt as if I were in a bad dream, and I kept asking God, 'Please, wake me up'.

Finally, the doctor came out. 'Your son is in a deep coma. His brain has been without oxygen long enough to suffer damage. To what extent we don't know.'

Mike and I turned and held each other, and prayed. Friends and relatives came to sit with us and pray. I sensed God's Holy Spirit surrounding us all.

Two days later the doctor came in with Jez's tests results. 'It's not promising,' he said. 'Your son is ninety percent brain dead. He might live on or die in a few days or weeks. We can't tell.'

I began sobbing. My friend Glenda put her arm around me. 'Michelle, you have to give Jez to God.'

I stared at her. *No,* I thought, *God has turned things around before for me. He can heal Jez too.*

Later that day as I held Jez's hand and talked to him, he drew my hand up to his head. My spirits soared. He could hear me! But every report was worse than the one before. On Sunday night, after Jez had been in a coma for four days, the doctor offered no hope. 'It could be,' he said, 'that the time may soon come when we should turn off his life-support system.' He looked up at us gravely. 'We could keep him going, or do you want us just to let him go? We will need to know your decision soon.'

Mike felt it would be best to let Jez go but I could not think of it.

Rachel, one of the many friends who had comforted us, stayed with me in the waiting room that night. I took off my shoes, lay down on a chair that converted into a bed, and finally went to sleep. But then I dreamed that I rose from my bed and walked into Jez's room. His body was attached to all sorts of needles and tubes. I leaned over and whispered in his ear, 'Jez, my little sweetheart, I have always tried to teach you to obey Mummy and Daddy. Well, now there is another who is calling you. I told you that above all others we are to obey our Heavenly Father. And if he is calling you, you must go to him.'

I picked up my child, and to my surprise, all the needles and tubes fell from him. I cradled his limp body in my arms. As I stood crying, I heard someone call my name. I looked up. It was Jesus! His eyes were full of compassion.

'Oh, Lord, heal him, please, whether it be by his living or going home with you,' I begged. But I already knew the answer. 'Lord,'

I continued, 'when Jez was born, we dedicated him to you. He is yours. I have always prayed that your will be done.'

He smiled. 'Daughter, I love you and will give you strength and comfort.'

I held Jez close, kissed him, and laid him at Jesus' feet. I stepped back and the Lord picked him up. Instantly Jez awoke. He looked up at the Lord, grinned and said, 'Hi, Jesus!'

The Lord held Jez out to me, and once more we played our little game. I touched his ear, his eye, his nose, mouth and cheek, and finished as always by saying, 'Mummy loves you; Jesus loves you.'

He kissed me and said, 'Jez loves you, and Jesus loves you too.'

Then Jesus, with Jez in his arms, began to walk out of the room. The Lord motioned me to come. We walked along the darkened hospital corridor, took the lift down to the lobby, and went past the reception desk to the double glass doors of the hospital entrance.

Outside, instead of the courtyard, there was a hill covered with deep green grass, and the sky was pure and clear.

I stood inside the door, watching in awe as Jesus set Jez down. He took off in a run for the hill, stopped, picked a flower and counted the petals, his voice crystal clear: 'One, two, three, nine!' (He still hadn't learned to count.)

'See,' Jesus said to me, 'he is alive. All who are in my care are alive and growing here.'

Then he and Jez walked over the hill together. Once, Jez looked back, smiled and called, 'Mummy, I love you and will always be at your side.' Then they were gone and I went back to sleep on my makeshift bed in the waiting room.

In the morning when I awoke, Rachel asked me a startling question: 'Did you know you were walking in your sleep last night?' She went on to tell me I had left the room, walked down the corridor and taken the lift.

'I couldn't have,' I insisted.

'No,' she said. 'You did some walking all right.' Rachel pointed to my feet. 'Okay, then explain why your shoes are on. You took them off when you went to bed. Now each is on the wrong foot.'

I looked down. She was right.

Then the night nurse stuck her head into the room and said to me, 'I hope I didn't disturb you last night when you were in Jez's room, praying.'

I was stunned. I had thought it all a dream. And yet . . .

Had it been only two months since I'd wondered if I'd had another dream – the music of the angels? But that music had been real. I had heard it, Jez had heard it. Why? Now, looking back, I knew. God was preparing us. But last night? It must have been the hand of God as well.

I got up and went into Jez's room, now half expecting to find his bed empty. But he was there, still connected to the tubes and the hissing machine. Yet something was different. As I looked down at him, somehow Jez was not the same. Then I knew Jez was gone; only his body lived on.

From that moment on I was at ease. I did not have to insist on keeping his life-support system running. I could let go.

But Mike and I didn't have to make that decision. In forty-eight hours Jez's heart stopped beating. And for the first time since the accident, he was smiling

A STREAM IN THE DESERT

by Betsy Young

A moment of heavenly tranquillity points to the future.

My husband was gravely ill. In desperation his doctors prescribed bypass heart surgery; a new and untested procedure at the time. Bob and I were both frightened and needed a reprieve.

A week before surgery we packed a picnic and, on a glorious California day, drove out to the Mojave Desert.

Bob loved the desert air; it was so dry and easy to breathe. We travelled aimlessly on back roads lined with desert flowers, yucca and the lovely paloverde tree. And then, on an off-road track, we chanced upon a path.

We left the car, and the path led us to a gentle stream of water. Such streams aren't unheard of in the Mojave in June, but they are very rare.

We sat beside the shaded pool. During the next few hours, picnicking, sunning, we were as happy as we'd ever been during our twenty-five years of marriage. The water, so unexpected, so soothing, soaked our hot feet, and especially pleased Bob. It reminded him of Psalm 23. 'He leads me to quiet pools of fresh water,' he quoted from memory.

And indeed, as we talked, the waters seemed to wash away our fears. Our souls were restored.

Reluctantly we left. But back at the car Bob realized he'd left his knife on a poolside stone and I walked back to retrieve it. There was the knife, glinting in the sun. But the brook, the pool ... they were gone. Where there had been water minutes earlier, there were now only stones and sand.

The following week Bob died on the operating table, his heart condition even worse than the doctors had suspected. I'm sure; though, that he died in peace, assured by our stream that he would dwell in the house of the Lord forever.

OUT OF OUR HANDS

by Roy Gilliland

Miracle in a wall of flames.

Seeing a car wreck on the six o'clock news is one thing, but being there at the scene of the accident is another. In seventeen years as a paramedic I've witnessed every kind of horror. We learn to expect the worst. Our real nightmare is fire. Paramedics are not fire fighters. We're trained – among other things – to rescue survivors from a vehicle and treat their injuries first, but if a car is in flames, it's a non-stop emergency. You just have to hope God's with you because there's not one moment to pray.

My partner Tom and I prided ourselves on suiting up in less than thirty seconds: protective pants and coat, helmet and fire-resistant gloves. One October afternoon in 1993 an urgent call came over the radio: 'Two-vehicle collision. Ferguson Road.'

'Let's go!' yelled Tom. We responded to the call. Tom had his gear on before we left the station. Mine was still stowed in a bag in the ambulance. Tom climbed into the driver's seat, and we proceeded to the accident location, just a few minutes north of town. *I'll set no records suiting up today,* I thought, reaching for my bag.

'Bad news, Roy,' Tom called out as he pulled our ambulance to a stop by the road. We were first on the scene. One car, its front end smashed, was on the highway, while off on the side of the road a white car was engulfed in flames. Fire roared into the sky. I caught my breath. Our puny ten-pound extinguisher was no match for a blaze like that.

'Two people are in front,' I said, spotting their silhouettes amid the flames. Tom ran to the driver's side of the burning car. I pulled on my gloves, grabbed my medical kit and got to the car seconds behind him.

Tom yanked on the door, desperate to reach the driver, whose stricken face was visible through the window. I could see the car's crumpled dashboard pushed into her body, trapping her. The door wouldn't budge. Just as I reached Tom's side the flames leaped into the front seat.

Panicked, the passenger shoved his door open, falling out on the ground. His clothes were on fire!

'Tom!' I yelled. The two of us carried the man away from danger. We pressed his chest and back with our protective gloves, smothering the flames. Then we heard a muffled bang. The car's windows had exploded from the heat. Tom ran back to the car while I opened my kit and began to treat the passenger's burns.

Sirens wailed as a fire engine screeched to a stop. Glancing up from my patient I saw Tom reach his arms through a wall of flames, into the car, trying to pull the trapped driver from her car.

'Out of the way!' shouted a firefighter, moving Tom aside. Positioning a hose, the firefighter directed a stream of water into the car. As the flames subsided, we could see that the driver was beyond help. *We do what we can,* I told myself sadly, returning to my patient. People say everything is in God's hands. In my line of work, that fact was sometimes hard to accept.

With the fire under control, we had our first chance to check the other car involved in the collision. The driver was crumpled in the seat in pain but conscious. As I was examining her I heard the thunder of an arriving helicopter, and a firefighter came up beside me to offer his help. 'Take care of this one,' I said. I went back to our injured passenger. Tom and I waited until our patient was turned over to the helicopter team.

We removed our protective clothing, and then drove back to the station to clean and restock our ambulance. I was reviewing the disturbing events of the day in my mind, still hoping for some kind of reassurance. Putting new sheets on the stretcher, I looked up and saw Tom. His face was pale.

'What's wrong?' I asked.

Without a word, Tom gave me his fire-resistant gloves. Three fingers of his left glove were gone, completely burned *off*. On his right glove, three fingers and the thumb were burned away.

'Are you okay?' I asked. Tom raised his hands and turned them palm up. I winced, expecting to see third-degree burns. But his hands were whole and healthy. I turned them over to examine the backs. Not a mark. No evidence of burns. I was speechless.

'That isn't all,' Tom said, motioning for me to follow him.

We walked around to the driver's side of the ambulance. Tom opened the door and pulled his protective coat from where he'd stowed it behind the seat. He stepped back, offering me the coat. I couldn't believe it! Both arms of his thick coat were charred black, clear up to the elbows.

'I watched you,' I said. 'You reached through the window of that car.'

'Fire all around me,' he agreed, nodding. 'A wall of fire.'

Tom pushed up his sleeves. Again, no burns. Not even the hair on his arms was singed. He'd reached through fire, but he was untouched. It was almost as if the laws of nature had changed.

'How could this be?' Tom asked.

I shrugged, and then spoke the answer that hovered in my mind: 'You were in God's hands.'

A GLIMPSE OF HEAVEN

by Janet Franck

To this day she doesn't understand why she was permitted to see the unseen.

I don't know why tragedy struck our family that bright October morning. Nor why I, of all people, should have been allowed that glimpse of Heaven. I only know that a presence greater than human was part of the experience from the beginning.

The strangeness started the evening before, when I allowed six-year-old Travis to play outside past his bedtime. I'd never done this before. Travis's two younger brothers were already asleep in bed, and he should have been too; he had to go to school in the morning, after all. But Tara, the little girl who lived across the street, was playing outdoors late too. Though Tara was a year older, there seemed to be a special bond between her and Travis. I heard their happy shouts as they played hide-and-seek under the enormous stars – just as I used to here in our little mountain town of Challis, Idaho.

And then, later, when I'd called him in at last and he was in his pyjamas, he'd suddenly grown so serious. 'Mummy?' Travis had finished his prayers as I sat on the edge of his bed. He took his hands and placed them tenderly on my cheeks. Such a solemn little face beneath the freckles!

'What, Babe?' I smiled.

'I . . . just love you, Mummy,' he said, searching my eyes. 'I just want you to know that I love you.'

The words remained with me, as I got ready for bed. Not that it was unusual for Travis to show affection. Little children who know Jesus seem to bubble over with love for the whole world, even at age five.

It was the intensity – almost the urgency – with which he'd said the words that was unlike him.

As I lay in bed that night, the sense that something out of the ordinary was about to happen stayed with me. Our house is small, and since my mother came to stay with us I've shared a bedroom with the children. I could hear their soft, restful breaths as they slept.

That wasn't what kept me awake. Nor was it the empty space beside me – my husband was now married to another. Yes, our family had certainly had its moments of pain, but our faith had brought us this far.

I thought back to that time four years before when I'd realized my need for God and invited him to take over my struggle. How magnificently he had! So much help had been lavished upon us going through the divorce, changed lifestyle and financial difficulties. From our pastor and church friends I'd gained strength and hope. But it was little freckle-faced Travis that brought me the day-by-day lessons.

'Why are you worried, Mummy?' Travis had said so many times, a hint of impatience in his wide brown eyes. 'You have Jesus. We'll get the money for that bill.' And we always did.

Two a.m. 'I love you, Mummy' still pealed in my ears like some distant, gentle bell. I remembered that as my closeness to God increased, my spirit would sometimes hear messages from him.

I am preparing Travis for something; I'd heard this silent voice tell me many times. And this did seem to be the case.

Hadn't there been that night a couple of months ago? I'd awakened before daylight and noticed Travis sitting on his bed. Just sitting, in the purple predawn.

'What's the matter, Babe?' I had asked him.

'Don't you see them?' He sounded disappointed.

'See what?'

'Those two angels.'

I breathed in sharply. I saw only the familiar room. The boy was wide-awake, perfectly calm. I asked him if he was afraid.

'No, Mummy,' he'd said. I waited by his bed a little while. Then he said, 'Okay, they're gone, you can go to bed now.' That was all. But thinking back on that experience, I felt again that sense of the extraordinary pressing close upon us.

The morning of 28 October dawned bright and still. There was the usual bustle of getting breakfast, finding socks that matched, pencils with erasers and so on. Ten minutes before the time he usually left to walk to school Travis became suddenly agitated.

'Mummy, I've got to go now.'

'Babe, it's early. You've got lots of time. Sit down.'

'I've got to go now! I've just got to!' Travis cried.

'Why?' I asked in bewilderment. He mumbled something about his teacher, about not being late. It didn't make sense. He was never late. 'Wait a few minutes,' I insisted. 'Finish your cocoa.'

'Mummy, please!' To my amazement big tears were rolling down his cheeks.

'All right, all right, go ahead,' I told him, shaking my head at the commotion. He dashed out the door, a hurrying little figure pulling on a tan jacket. Across the street, little Tara was coming down her pathway. I saw the two children meet and set off toward Main Street together.

Five minutes later I was clearing away the breakfast dishes when it happened.

A shudder of the floor beneath me, then a hideous screech of writhing wood. There had never been an earthquake in Challis, but I knew we were having an earthquake now. I ran from the house calling over my shoulder, 'I've got to get to Travis.'

I was at the driveway when another tremor flung me against the car. I waited till the earth stopped heaving, and then climbed into the driver's seat.

I'd gone two blocks when I saw a woman standing beside a pile of rubble on the pavement, the debris of a collapsed storefront.

The look on her face was one of nightmare horror. Unrolling the window, I was surprised at the calmness of my voice as I asked, 'Was someone . . . caught?'

'Two children,' the white face said thinly. 'One in a tan jacket. . .'

I drove swiftly on. Past people running towards the damaged building. Around the corner, to the school. Oh, I knew. I knew already. But maybe – please God! – maybe farther down the street there'd be two children standing bewildered at a kerbside. There were not, of course. I drove back to the rubble heap.

Then a numb blur of events: police, firemen, people struggling with the debris. Identification. Arms around me. I was at the hospital. I was being driven home. I was in my living room again. My mother was there, and I was telling her and my two little boys what had happened. Mother was praying.

Suddenly, as I sat there in the living room, perhaps even in mid-sentence – I don't know how long it took – I was being lifted right out of the room, lifted above it all, high into the sky, and placed by a beautiful gate. A cluster of happy people stood within the gate. In utter amazement I began recognizing the youthful, robust faces: Dad, my favourite aunt, Grandpa . . . and in the centre of them all, a radiant form. As I watched, he stretched out his hands to welcome a child, who was approaching. A smiling boy dressed in what seemed to be an unbleached muslin tunic over long trousers of the same homespun-looking fabric. Travis ran forward and grasped the hand of Jesus, looking up at him with eager brown eyes. The cluster of people welcomed my son, and he seemed to recognize them, although some he had never met. The joyful group turned to leave, Travis suddenly turned his shining face toward me, 'It's really great here, Mummy.'

'I know, Babe.' My throat felt choked, and I don't know whether I spoke aloud or not.

'I really like it here.'

'I know.'

'Mummy . . . I don't want to go back.'

'It's okay, Babe.' And it was okay, in that transcendent moment nothing I could ever do, nothing that could ever happen here on earth, could make Travis as happy as I saw him right then. When I looked around me, I was back in my home.

That's where the long battle of grief was fought, of course, in the kitchen with its empty chair, in the bedroom where he'd said his goodnight prayers, and the garden where he'd played hide-and-seek. Transcendent moments do not last – not for us on earth. Three years have passed since the day of the earthquake, passed among the daily routines of cleaning, cooking, chauffeuring, praying.

But neither do such moments fade.

That scene at heaven's threshold is as vivid in each detail today as in the measureless instant when I was allowed to see a glimpse of heaven's glory.

LOST IN THE WHIRLPOOL

by Donald Shaffer

The raging torrent roared into a hole forty feet deep, yet he knew he had to plunge in.

The blaring ring of the telephone jarred me awake. I looked at the clock – 3.15 a.m. On the other end of the phone I heard the voice of Bill Barnhart, Somerset's fire chief.

'Don,' he said, 'there's a report of a drowning down at Swallow Falls . . . a little boy. They need some people down there to help. Can you get your scuba boys together?'

Oh, brother, I thought, *just what I need at three o'clock in the morning.* But as a volunteer scuba diver, I knew the commitment I'd made.

'I'll see what I can do,' I answered. Surprisingly, especially since it was a Sunday, I was able to round up eight other divers, and an hour later, still rubbing sleep from our eyes, we met at the base.

We were briefed on the facts. The boy, ten, had been wading with his father early Saturday evening in the treacherous part of the river, just above Swallow Falls. Suddenly, the boy had been scooped up by the raging current and swept over the hills into a whirlpool forty feet deep. His father dived into the raging pool below the falls in an attempt to reach the waterfall, but was unsuccessful and barely escaped the torrents of water himself. Then he organized a search party along the shore, but again to no avail.

I shook my head sadly at the thought of the little fellow's fate. It sounded hopeless. Then I heard the chief say something that made me realize why we were all there in the middle of the night.

'Since no body has been found, there's a chance the boy may still be alive somewhere,' Bill said. 'Until we find him we can't be sure he's gone.'

Riding in our rescue truck on the hour-and-a-half trip over the wilderness to that isolated area, I thought about the several drownings near Swallow Falls in recent years. While I had never visited the falls before, I have heard tales of their ferocity, especially at this time of year, the high-water season.

Then I thought about the boy. Was it possible he was still alive? In the darkness of the truck, I shivered. I teach Sunday school and try to believe what I teach. Yet, at the same time, prayer comes awfully hard for me. It has always been a struggle for me to ask God for something. Yet travelling down the back roads that morning, I felt a great need to pray. Closing my eyes, I murmured, 'God, if that boy is still alive, all I ask is that we be given the chance to rescue him.'

We reached Swallow Falls just as the sun was coming up. One look at the place confirmed my worst fears. About ten feet high and a hundred feet across, the falls tumbled down with a deafening roar into a lake-sized stream – the rain-swollen river. Near the middle of the stream was an ugly whirlpool, sucking and swishing around like a glint funnel, an awesome sight.

It seemed foolhardy to enter water like that. Standing on a rock, I watched in silence until my back-up diver, Rick Ross, appeared alongside me.

'Don, I'm really scared,' Rick said. He didn't have that much experience as a diver; none of us really did. I had taken up scuba diving only seven years before after a holiday in the Bahamas. Once I got involved in the sport, I was hooked. I'd taken lessons and then joined the scuba rescue team the summer before. But I'd never had to save anybody and certainly had never ventured into water like that. 'Rick,' I said, 'I'm scared too. But we can't let our fear beat us.'

Our first plan was to have me swim into the falls. With my diving gear on, I attacked the pounding water four times. Each time I was beaten down and thrown back into the stream.

Next, we strung a rope, shoreline to shoreline, across the top of the falls. Attaching another rope to that line in a T fashion, I stayed in the water and tried to guide my way through the falls. This too proved fruitless; the charging water bounced me around like a piece of sponge.

We were discouraged now and running out of ideas. Working quickly, we next tied a rope to a rock upstream, above the falls. Hanging on the rope, I pulled myself through the falls to the rock face in back. I felt my feet land on a thin ledge of rock. Just then the rope locked in the rock face above me, so I had to let go of the rope, leaving myself with no means of getting out. Completely out of sight now, I had no trouble imagining what the other men must have thought when they saw that lonely rope float by without me.

Inching my way along the ledge behind the falls, in water up to my chest, I found myself in an eerie corridor, walled in by an ear-shattering cascade. All my shouts, I knew, would be in vain.

Suddenly I looked up and gasped. *The boy!* There, on a small ledge about one foot above the water level was the boy. At the startling sight of him, I gave a noiseless cheer and felt goose bumps crisscross my arms and legs.

Wearing only a bathing suit, the boy was lying on his side on a stone notch carved out by the force of the water. Apparently, after going over the falls, he had been swept up in there by the whirlpool. It was an incredible landing spot, only big enough for one small person to recline on. *Surely,* I thought, *God's hand must have placed him there.*

My heart was pounding as I neared the boy. His eyes were closed, *If he opens them,* I thought, *he's going to see me and panic.* Here I was in this spooky place, all decked out like a creature from outer space. It would be enough to scare anybody, let alone a little boy who hadn't seen another soul for twelve hours.

Trying to keep cool, I approached the boy. Quickly he rose up, frightened. I worked my way over on the ledge and put my arm around him.

'Are you all right?' I asked.

'Yes,' he said, his blue eyes glowing brightly. He was cold, but seemed calm.

'Okay,' I said, knowing that we seemed to be trapped. 'We're going to ask God to get us out.'

The boy needed no coaxing. Turning over, he put his palms together and bowed his head. I did the same.

'Dear God,' I said, 'please help us to get out of this alive.'

I knew it was one thing to ask God for help, but it was another to actually survive. My first thought was that perhaps we could 'buddy breath' our way out – that is, pass my air regulator back and forth. I had to reject that idea, though. It just didn't seem like we'd have the time or be able to coordinate the action. Our only answer was for me to use the regulator and hold the boy at the same time. He might swallow some water, but I hoped not too much.

Holding the boy in my right arm, I eased myself along the ledge the way I came in. I was hoping to find a place in the falls where the water pressure was weakest. As we went, occasionally being blasted by a sheet of water, I had to admire the boy for acting so calmly.

A few moments later, the ledge I was standing on dropped and my air tank caught on the upper part of the rock behind me. We couldn't go forward or backward. I knew what that meant. We'd have to go straight through the full force of Swallow Falls.

I looked at the boy. He was quiet. I pointed to the roaring tumult. 'We're going to have to swim through that,' I said. 'Take a deep breath.'

'Okay,' he said. Again I was amazed by his courage. He swung his body around to face me, locked his hands around my neck, his legs around my waist. With all my power I pushed off with my legs into the thundering water and in direct line of the whirlpool.

As we struck the main thrust of the falls, we were driven down, down, down into a swirling, bubbling blackness. After about fifteen seconds of being pitched about, I began kicking my flippers desperately. It was a race against time; I had to get the boy's head above the surface.

Fighting my way up, I took the boy by the waist and with every ounce of my strength I thrust him upward in a catapult motion. I was suddenly glad for all those years I had worked in the concrete business. Hauling heavy blocks and stone by hand had given me power in my arms, but even so, I was amazed at all that instant strength.

As the boy shot up past me, my regulator was knocked loose and water began pouring down my throat. It didn't matter, for suddenly, I too was rising to the surface.

When my head broke the water I heard wild yelling and screaming. I looked around and saw a diver jump from a rock and grab the boy. We'd made it! We had missed the whirlpool by inches. In a few seconds a rowboat was by my side. Still gagging water, I grabbed onto it. I felt a strange mixture of weariness and joy.

Later, when the boy's father reached me by telephone to express his gratitude, I learned that the family had been visiting Swallow Falls when the near-tragedy occurred.

The boy's name, I learned, was Richard Bouchard. It wasn't too long before I got a chance to visit Richard. He's a great little guy who loves games, and, believe it or not, swimming.

Though neither of us really mentioned the rescue when we talked, I know neither of us will ever forget it. It's an experience both of us will always cherish, something that comes along once in a lifetime. God, in bringing two strangers together in an improbable and dangerous place, heard our plea and gave each of us the courage to find the way out. Richard and I will always be bound by that struggle, but even more, we'll be tied by a knot of faith that can't be broken.

NO LONGER AFRAID

by Linda Hanick

Letting go is often the hardest thing.

Our daughter, Erica, came into this world blind.

Later, grave medical problems followed. Erica was almost four when it became clear she was dying as Jack and I kept vigil at her hospital bedside, our prayers for healing gradually became prayers for wisdom and acceptance.

Then Jack looked at me searchingly. 'Linda,' he said, 'we should do more than pray to God about Erica. We need to talk to Erica about God.'

I knew he was right. Erica was afraid, afraid of dying. Despite her pain, I sensed she was holding on to us because we were the surest love she knew.

Cupping her tiny hands, we told her that God's love was so much greater than ours, and that she had to try to let go – of this hospital room, this bed, even us.

'Where you are going is a safe place, more beautiful and full of love than anything you've ever known ...'

In my mind I saw Erica running and skipping over emerald grass through fields of rainbow coloured flowers. Her golden hair blazed in the sunlight. Her voice was laughter and her eyes were like the sky, cloudless and blue. She was no longer blind.

A nurse came by to record Erica's vital signs. Though it was clear Erica's physical condition remained the same, I sensed a change, something deep in her spirit.

I was about to tell Jack what I saw in mind when he said, 'You know, just before the nurse came in I had the strongest image. I saw Erica, so vividly, skipping and running across a field of beautiful flowers. She was laughing. And her eyes were clear and blue as the sky.

THE GATEWAY

by Martin Bauer

I should be dead, I thought.

When it was all over, the doctors said I had been lucky to survive. But now, over a decade later, I still can't help feeling lucky to have come so close to death and returned.

I was nineteen at the time. At dawn on that fateful day a friend had dropped me off at the wooded border of my old summer camp. Unseen, I made my way to Black Pond, a glistening body of water the camp shared with the public. My mood was mischievous, for I was about to work my way around a promise I'd made to John, the camp's director.

John had been forced to quarantine the grounds because of a throat epidemic, and he told me I wasn't allowed to visit. Knowing how much I wanted to see my brother Andy, John extracted my solemn word: I swore I wouldn't visit the camp. But it occurred to me that were I to go for a swim alongside the camp's waterfront and visit from there, I'd technically be within the bounds of the agreement. A friend would get word of my plan to Andy.

That's how I found myself at the water's edge. The campers wouldn't arrive on their side of the pond for another hour, so I decided to take a short hike to Hilltop, an overnight campsite. Dominated by towering white pines, Hilltop was covered by grass and soft pine needles. It was one of my favourite spots in the area.

As I hiked a side path leading to Hilltop I broke into a sweat, though the air retained its morning chill. Overhead the treetops swayed in a steady breeze, and I was grateful to reach the cool crest. Since it would be a while before any camper came down to the waterfront, I decided to climb a tree to take in the view. I selected the tallest pine in the area.

I was careful. The lower limbs of a white pine, though appearing sturdy, are often dead; the bark can be rotten and slippery. I climbed in close, where the branches met the trunk, so there was less chance of their shearing off.

At the top, the breeze was strong and delightful, blowing through my hair and over my skin. I could see the camp boathouse, nearly three quarters of a mile away. No one was there, so I relaxed in the coolness for about five minutes. I'd begun to climb down when I heard my brother's call:

'Maaartiiinnn!'

I laughed and climbed up near the top again. So much for the idea of a surreptitious visit! Andy was calling from the waterfront.

'Aaannndyy!' I hailed him back.

'Where aaarrre yooouuu?' he cried.

I climbed farther up, as high as I dared. The wind was whipping my words around so much, I wasn't sure Andy could hear me. 'Hillltooop!' I yelled, waving, and was rewarded to see him jump up and wave in return. We hollered back and forth like two kids with a new toy.

Eventually, we arranged a time and place to meet along the water's edge later in the morning, then shouted goodbye.

With my hands clamped tightly around different branches, I moved one foot down. At that moment, the branches I grasped suddenly snapped off with a *crack*. I was instantly sent hurtling through the air, some sixty-five feet above the ground.

The treetop rushed away. Flailing arms and legs, I crashed through the branches, grabbing desperately for a handhold, anything to break my fall. Then the lights went out.

I float in a world of grey. My eyes are open, my sight clear. Am I asleep and dreaming? If so, it is by far the most vivid dream I've ever had. I do not know where I am. This world is grey but it has depth and is distinct, like the overcast greyness of clouds rolling over the mountains of northern New England.

There is something to my left. I turn to look, but can only do so slowly. As I turn, a golden light appears. Gradually, it pushes the grey away. My curiosity intensifies as the light grows brighter, but try as I might I cannot shift faster to see its source. Slowly, ever so slowly, I understand that what is out of sight is not a something but a someone – a presence, radiating a tremendous force of warmth and love, divine love. Joy swells in my heart, and I know this is no dream. My excitement soars as I struggle to reach the light so full of life and peace.

And with this effort, my legs find movement, as if finally freed from mud. Suddenly the light and the grey fade away.

I awoke and found myself lying on my back in a bed of grass and soft pine needles, looking up through the branches at the sun. The vision was gone, but the swell of euphoria remained.

Several minutes passed before I realized what had happened to me. *I should be dead,* I thought. But incredibly, this fact seemed relatively insignificant compared to what I had just experienced. It was astonishingly clear that I had come to a doorstep few see but once: the gateway between this life and the next, a portal from where I had glimpsed the all-loving presence of God.

Reassured, I closed my eyes again and slept. For the next five hours I faded in and out of consciousness. The experience of the light did not return. I felt no pain. In fact, I felt wonderfully relaxed; but I knew that this was the result of shock.

I managed to take stock of myself. My right eye was swollen shut, and I could see only slightly out of my left. Cuts and scrapes from my six-story plunge through the brittle branches had left me covered in dried blood. My hands were numb and my left wrist was bent at an odd angle. When I tried to sit up, a searing bolt of pain shot through me, shattering my tranquillity. I cried out, then lost consciousness.

When I awoke again I began to comprehend how dire my circumstances were. Andy hadn't seen me fall, and as a cabin leader he'd be too busy to be overly concerned when I missed our rendezvous. He wouldn't worry until later, maybe when it was too late. Since the camp was quarantined, no one would be out in the woods. I began to panic at the thought that there was no way for anyone to know my situation.

Then I remembered the experience with the light. Gradually, my fears subsided. Would I have been drawn back from the gateway had I not been meant to live?

It was strange, this comfort. When I was a boy and people said, 'Pray to God,' I didn't understand. I tried, but something was missing. In my teens, throughout school, life was often unclear to me and I wondered why adults did not have all the answers. I realized then that such responses were not always spoken, that adults often didn't know any more than youngsters.

Without words, at the gateway, an answer had been given to me: There was a time to live and a time to die, and my time to die had not yet come. Life was a precious gift. And however impossible it seemed, somehow I had to make my way back down to the pond and get help.

Little by little, I managed to sit up and move my uninjured left leg into a kneeling position. Then, hugging and pulling with my upper arms on the tree I'd fallen from, I painfully inched my way up until I was standing relatively upright. I rested, panting for breath. The effort had exhausted me. But I was elated.

Soon the panic returned. Where was the path down to the pond? With my vision blurred I did not know which direction to go. I was disoriented by fatigue and pain. *Dear Lord,* I cried silently, throwing my head back. And in so doing I found my answer – the most reliable means of natural orientation staring me right in the face. With the sun as my guide, I triangulated the direction of the pond. Despite my blurred sight, I found the path in seconds. Hobbling, I painfully covered the several hundred yards down to the water, where my calls for help were eventually heard.

I learned later that I had broken both my arms, fractured my right hip, shattered the bone around my right eye, severely bruised four ribs on the right side of my chest and nearly punctured a lung. I am glad I did not know all of this at the time. It might have tested my resolve.

Yet when I think about it, I tend to believe it wouldn't have made any difference. My brief encounter at the gateway would have sustained me no matter what, even as it sustains me today. For this I give thanks to God.

HERE FOR GOOD

by Grace Dodds

If you could have known me, the sort of person I was before!

I was in labour, for the first time, and it was an extremely difficult labour. I was thirty, and the cervix wasn't dilating properly, and nothing was happening. This had just been going on and on and on, and it was excruciating. I was starting to drift in and out of consciousness and the doctors were very panicked. They kept coming in and listening to the foetal heartbeat and checking my pulse.

I think that's fairly normal, but all of a sudden there seemed to be a lot of panic. Nurses were wheeling things in, my husband was shooed out, I was sort of drifting in and out and suddenly I wasn't there anymore. I mean, up until then there had been an awareness of what was going on around me, even though I'd been drifting in and out of blackness. But the last thing I remember before I did move, or had the sensation of movement, was hearing someone cry out, 'We're losing her.'

Then suddenly I was somewhere else.

I recall a sensation of movement out beyond myself, as if I'd left something behind. And I seemed to move through a portal. There was a glow, but I didn't seem to stop and think, there was no thought, there was no 'Will I, won't I?' Just suddenly, I found myself in a place, a real place, and I was standing just beyond the portal and looking around me. There was an intensity of colour. It was green, an intense emerald green. There were gentle rolling hills, there were no crags, no sharp edges, nothing that was cruel, nothing that was other than gentle.

The sky was intense blue, the scene was gently rolling, and there seemed to be figures, grouped, almost a theatrical grouping, like a stage set. And at first they were just amorphous, shadowy figures. I was peripherally but intensely aware of a grouping on my right, ahead of me, but I hadn't really looked at it.

I knew it was there but it was not impinging on my consciousness too much at that stage – I was too busy looking the other way. And as I looked one of the figures seemed to resolve itself, and I thought, *I know that face,* and I suddenly realized, *Oh God, it's my Aunty Hannah,* who died eleven years ago. And then I saw my Uncle Abraham, who died before I was born, and I knew them. They were not speaking, their mouths weren't moving, but they were there. I knew they were there to see me, and they knew me, even though they had never met me.

My granny, who I'd never met, my grandfather, all the people I've never known and even those I'd known a bit who'd died many years before, or who'd even died recently, were there. Then I turned and I looked at this figure standing next to me – it was my father.

My dad died when I was sixteen. I was a very rebellious teenager and we were always at loggerheads. The day he died, we were moving – we'd sold the house and we were going to move into a flat – and he and I had a towering row. I said to him, 'I hate you,' the normal teenage ugly thing. Anyway, he went to the flat with the movers for the last time, saying he'd come back and get me later on. I was waiting for Dad to come back and the afternoon wore on and there was no sign of him. It was growing dusk when I saw a police car going past. Suffice to say Dad had had a coronary. He died very suddenly, there were no saying goodbyes, no chance to say, 'Dad, I'm really sorry, I didn't mean that. I do love you.' It was so quick and he was gone. I never really was able to mourn properly and was dashed off to Sydney to live with my mother. It was all very practical: 'Now, don't cry. You'll be all right.'

But I always had this terrible sense that I never had a chance to say goodbye or that I was sorry.

And then standing in that place, it went through my mind, *Is this real or is this my imagination because it's what I want to have happened?* It's really peculiar, but I actually thought that. *Am I doing this within myself because it's what I want?*

And then Dad spoke to me, although there was no speaking – his mind spoke to me. And he said, 'No, honey,' because that was his name for me. 'Honey, you're not imagining. It's not coming from you, you're with me and this is our time to talk.' We did talk, laid the ghosts to rest. As I looked down there was my dog Lucky. He died when I was very young, and he was there too. Of course now if I were to go to the same place, my German shepherd would be there too. I'm quite looking forward to seeing Razzy again. Sounds crazy, doesn't it?

I didn't have any sense of time, I don't know how long it was, but we talked about all sorts of things. And I said to him, 'You must wonder what I've been doing, or you must sometimes feel angry with me.'

And he said, 'No. Here, what goes on in the world has no meaning.' He said, 'We're here to care for you, we're here to take you on.'

And then there was a sense of drawing back, and I panicked and said, 'Dad, I don't want to go!'

He said, 'You have to go, it's not your time yet, you must go back. You're going to have a son, and you'll have to bring this boy up, bring him up by yourself.'

It's as though a part of me has been changed. My whole outlook on life has changed so drastically. Before that time I'd always been scared of death, terrified of going into a world of pain. I used to think you'd have the sensation of suffocating, choking, pain. I really didn't know, but I was terrified. But now I know you go to that place. Now I believe death is just another part of human development – you're born, you live, you marry, you have children, you die – it's just another step on the road. I'm still formulating ideas – I'm not sure exactly what happens, and that's something I guess that I'll find out when I get there. But I'm not frightened at all.

Up until the time of that experience, I had been fascinated by the esoteric or, rather, the mystical. I'd searched down many paths. I'd read widely on Buddhism, studied Catholicism and looked into all sorts of different areas, for instance, spiritualism. But after that experience, I felt I had the answer. I was brought up as a Jew, but now I'm not interested in names and tags anymore. I now believe the most important thing is how I feel about myself, how much I like myself, how much I care about the people around me and the world I live in.

If you could have known me, the sort of person I was before! I've never been a bad person, or immoral, or anything like that, but I was totally irresponsible – not bad, just impulsive. If I wanted to do something, I'd do it. But after that experience, I had a mission; I was given a job to do. It's as simple as that. Up until then, life was aimless – I was living for myself but I came back with a sense of purpose.

Suddenly I had to bring up this child alone, I had a responsibility. I had a reason to be, a reason to do everything. I had never held down a job. I'd knocked around and travelled all over the place and nothing meant anything. But afterwards, it was completely different. It was like pulling up a shade, and looking outside. I can't explain it. Everything completely changed overnight.

Suddenly I became a very responsible adult person, and I remember my mother saying, 'Something has changed you so much.' I tried to tell her about it, but she just said, 'Don't be silly!'

My lifestyle today is responsible and very caring. I'm now a personnel consultant, and I have a reputation for being very different from other consultants – very, very empathic. Without people telling me, I seem to understand what they're trying to say. And that's not trumpet sounding, but just an understanding. I think I get more out of what I'm doing because I'm helping. I'm doing something for other people rather than just doing something for me.

After my near-death experience I didn't just grow up – the fabric of my being was rewoven.

STRONG AND FREE

by Lois Lemieux

I couldn't believe it. My little son, who had lain weakly on the pillow for days, now grasped my arm urgently, and his grip was strong.

I put on my coat, picked up my car keys and turned towards my son Jarrod's bedroom to say goodbye before leaving. As I came down the hall, I could hear Bonnie Rutherford talking to him. Bonnie was a volunteer trained by the hospice, a service for patients in the last stages of illness.

'How are you doing today, Jarrod?' Bonnie was asking him cheerfully.

'I'm sick of it,' he answered tiredly.

I leaned my head against the doorframe and shut my eyes tight. Jarrod was the youngest of my five children. I knew, and Jarrod knew, that he was dying. Day by day he was losing ground to the incurable disease he'd been born with.

So how could a mother put on her coat, get in her car and drive down to her job while her thirteen-year-old son was suffering?

I could do it because I had to. I could go off to my job because Jarrod and I had to have periods of relief from the emotional intensity that was always there when we were together. And I could leave him because the hospice service made it possible. These incredible people had organized a complete team, including medical professionals, helpers from community agencies, clergy, and friends. They were all helping us care for Jarrod in the comfort and privacy of his own home.

And yet, of course, I never really left this son of mine. He was always in my thoughts and my prayers. Like an endless thread the same words rolled through my mind: *God, please, God, when the end comes, please don't let Jarrod be afraid.*

'I know how you feel, Jarrod,' Bonnie was saying.

Her tone was quiet, quietly understanding. 'My sister was paralysed and she had a lot of pain. But right at the end, when I was holding her hand, I saw her smile...'

I closed my eyes more tightly. Jarrod hadn't smiled for three weeks now.

'Right before she died she was happy,' Bonnie went on. 'My sister seemed to be seeing things I couldn't see and she was so delighted. She said that she could walk again. You'll be like that, Jarrod,' Bonnie continued. 'You'll have a new body. You'll be able to run again!'

I peeped at Jarrod. He was listening, his blue eyes wide in his pallid face.

'And when you see my sister in heaven, Jarrod,' Bonnie concluded, patting his thin arm, 'you just run up and hug her and tell her for me that I still love her and that I took care of you, will you?'

Jarrod nodded. He seemed to relax against the pillow. Bonnie was giving him a mission. Now I went in. I kissed him goodbye. 'I love you, Mum,' he said weakly.

'I love you too, Jarrod,' I whispered, and left for work. We were into another day. How many more would there be? How many more opportunities would we have to build his courage?

Until fourteen months earlier, January 1980, Jarrod had managed to live a fairly normal life. In spite of frequent bouts with pneumonia, a chronic cough, special pills and three weeks in the hospital every year for treatments, my blond, blue-eyed son grew up pretty much like any little boy.

At six, he was able to start school. Like so many children, he loved animals, and his bedroom was cluttered with stuffed dogs and bears and seals and plastic models of horses. Animal posters decorated the walls, along with his own pencil drawings of elk and deer.

Most poignant to me was the fact that Jarrod – a child with a severely limited life expectancy – developed a special love for endangered species, in particular the eagle and the wolf. That love was the reason we let Jarrod have a wolf-husky pup of his own. Skyak, as Jarrod named him, was never far from his side. Life was busy. It became easy to avoid thinking about what the doctors had told me soon after Jarrod was born. Most children with cystic fibrosis don't live past their teen years.

Not long before Jarrod's twelfth birthday in January 1980, his paediatrician, Liz Gunderson, felt he ought to go elsewhere for more specialized treatment. The doctor there really levelled with him about the seriousness of his disease. He told us he thought Jarrod could live only six more months.

Jarrod came home with a portable oxygen apparatus that could travel around with him. We put an oxygen concentrator beside his bed for him to use during the night. He began to miss school more often and needed more and more supplemental oxygen. In July Dr Gunderson referred us to the hospice, and they assigned a patient care coordinator to our family to line up the helpers and counsellors we would need – medical, psychological, spiritual, social and economic.

The team that the hospice assembled for Jarrod had close to twenty-five members – everyone from respiratory therapists and social workers to a clergyman from the Plymouth Congregational Church, Pastor Bill Burkhardt.

With the encouragement of these caring people, Jarrod had enrolled in the sixth grade in September, even though he was self-conscious about being 'different' and having to use his portable oxygen supply. He'd kept up with his interests by attending a hunter-safety training programme. He'd even taken part in a documentary television film about cystic fibrosis.

Jarrod's thirteenth birthday was on 18 January 1981. His brother, sister, stepfather and I put on an open house, and every one of his

hospice team came. By then, the same bond that had grown between Jarrod and those who spent time with him had also sprung up
among themselves. Though Jarrod was weak physically, it was a day
of celebrating strength and faith, a day of gratitude for each other.

Two months after his birthday, Jarrod needed to be on oxygen
all the time. He'd had to give up school. He'd lost the independence
of walking through the house and needed support as he stepped
into a wheelchair to go from his bed to the bathroom.

The sunny glint was gone from his hair and his eyes seemed to
grow larger in his pale face. Lately I'd wake up at night and hear
him talking out loud to God. 'Why don't you take me?' he'd say. 'I
want to go.'

March 20. Two days had passed since I had heard Bonnie's talk
with Jarrod. Now Pastor Burkhardt came to our house with a
surprise. He'd been visiting Jarrod every week, and knowing of
his keen interest in eagles, the pastor brought with him Vince
Yannone, a man who worked at the Wildlife and Parks Department. Mr Yannone had brought an injured golden eagle that someone had taken to the refuge.

Jarrod's mouth dropped when Mr Yannone carefully lifted the
eagle from his box cage. He leaned forward from his pillow on the
living room sofa, his eyes as bright and intense as the eagles.
'Hurry! Get my camera!' he called to Lynn, one of the hospice
workers.

The bird's great talons were shackled so that he could not
escape, but the strength in those claws was evident as they
clutched Mr Yannone's gloved hands. Then, as if responding to a
silent command, the eagle stretched his great wings across our
living room to their full six-foot span. Almost breathless with awe,
I turned to Jarrod. For the first time in weeks, he was smiling –
a smile that even the oxygen tubes wreathing his face couldn't hide.
He buffeted Mr Yannone with questions for almost an hour.

At bedtime, as usual, Jarrod and I prayed the Lord's Prayer
together, a ritual he had always loved. He also liked to have me
read to him from the Bible. And this night, I knew exactly where

to turn. Opening the pages at Isaiah 40 I read: 'But those that trust in the Lord shall have their strength renewed. They will rise on wings like eagles; they will run and not get weary, they will walk and not grow weak.'

March 21. A Saturday. I didn't have to go to work. I was fixing breakfast when I heard Jarrod laughing and talking loudly. I hurried to his room, bringing him a dish of cereal, but he put the bowl aside.

'I'm big!' he announced, glancing around the room happily. 'Look how big I am, Mum!'

I couldn't believe it. My little son, who had lain weakly on the pillow for days, now grasped my arm urgently, and his grip was strong.

'How big are you, Jarrod?' I asked, astonished by his robust touch.

'I'm big,' he told me, 'big as God.'

His voice had been thin and tired for the past month, but now it was full of vigour. Then I realized that this morning he wasn't coughing!

'And I'm strong,' Jarrod was assuring me.

'How strong are you, Jarrod?'

His eyes were darting here and there around the room and I wondered if he might be delirious. Still, his happiness thrilled me.

'*This* strong,' Jarrod replied, picking up an empty tissue box and ripping it down the side. He *was* strong.

I had to run to turn off a burner on the stove. When I came back, I thought at first that Jarrod was asleep. He was slumped forward and he had spilled cereal down his front. I reached out to tug off his pyjama top. He wasn't really asleep after all, for his arms were limp as I helped him out of his shirt.

'I love you, Jarrod,' I told him softly.

He didn't reply. Suddenly I realized that all I had prayed for was happening. Jarrod was breaking out of his body, no longer hackled by coughing or pain. I had seen him laughing and vigorous again. God had let me see him free and whole – and fearless.

In the quiet room, I heard the hushed sound of oxygen escaping from Jarrod's breathing tubes. Its gentle whisper told me that he had gone. It was over. A strong young eagle was rising, soaring.

4

WHEN FAMILIES
CAN BE FUN

*Life affords no greater responsibility,
no greater privilege, than the raising
of the next generation.*

C. Everett Koop

MOTORIZED MOTHER

by Patricia Lorenz

How drivetime became prime time.

'I'm tired of spending my whole life in that car,' I grumbled, scowling as I grabbed the car keys off the kitchen counter. My son Michael had just reminded me that we had to go out to buy his football boots that evening.

'I'm averaging two hundred miles a week just driving you kids to games, lessons, rehearsals, shopping, and taking you to friends' houses! Two hundred miles a week and nobody cares!' My voice faded when I realized nobody was listening.

As a single parent, I was the one to do the driving whenever the four kids needed to be driven somewhere around our sprawling twenty-eight square miles of countryside.

'Mum, don't forget there's the dance at school tonight,' Julie reminded.

Back home from that jaunt, I collapsed in front of the TV to read the newspaper, when suddenly six-year-old Andrew was at my side. 'Mummy, can we go to the shops now?'

'No, dear, not now,' I said wearily.

'But your birthday's tomorrow,' Andrew whimpered

Ah, yes, my birthday. I had forgotten I'd promised to take him shopping. He'd been saving his pocket money to buy me a present. He'd decided upon earrings and expected me to help pick them out.

'All right, Andrew,' I said. 'Let me put my shoes back on and get ready. We'll go now.' How do you say no to such a big heart implanted in such a little body? At the store we browsed among the carousels of earrings, giggling at the strange ones, oohing and aahing at the beautiful ones. Andrew pointed to a pair he liked. I told him they were beautiful.

They were also on sale for three pounds, a pound less than what he had clutched in his cowboy coin purse.

Knowing he'd made up his mind, I said, 'Andrew, decide what you want to do while I go over here and buy socks for Michael.' I knew he needed to be alone.

From the next aisle I could hear his pride-filled voice saying, 'Yes, please,' when the lady asked him if he needed a box for the earrings. 'It's my Mum's birthday and I'm going to wrap them in red paper with white hearts.'

After a stop for an ice cream, we headed home, and Andrew disappeared into his room with the red paper and a roll of tape.

'Get your pyjamas on, love, then come to my room and we'll read your bedtime story in my bed.'

When he jumped in the bed, Andrew snuggled close to me.

'Mummy, this is the happiest day of my life!'

'Why is that, honey?'

'It's the first time I've ever been able to do anything for *you!*' Then his arms surrounded me in a spontaneous bear hug.

While Andrew plodded out loud through one of his primary school reading books, I thought about my own acts of giving. I was always *giving* to my four children – especially behind the wheel of that car. Yet somehow I was never really happy about it.

Later I tucked this little boy with the big heart into his bed. 'What about prayers, Mum?'

I'd forgotten. 'Oh, of course, love.'

I held Andrew's small hands in mine and thanked God for my son, and for all my children. I asked God to help me be a happier, more cheerful mother.

Later I looked up the verse that had been running through my head, the one about God loving a cheerful giver. Having read it through again, then and there I decided to stop being such a grouch about all the driving.

And as I became something I thought I'd never be, a cheerful chauffeur, I found that I was listening to things I'd never quite heard before. On the way to band or drum lessons, Michael, age fourteen, thought out loud about whether he should go out for more football practice. He also told me about the girl in his class who had called him the night before, discussed whether he'd get a job after school and talked about what he wanted to do with his life.

When Julie, age fifteen, was in the car with me, she bubbled on and on about the latest antics in her hockey squad, about the boy who'd asked her to his house, about the student council fundraising idea and about getting extra help in maths.

On the way to Jeanne's piano lessons, confirmation classes and a special event at the local art school, we talked about where she wanted to go to college, what was happening in her art classes and why she felt her social life was at a standstill.

Amazed by what I'd missed as a cranky mum honking and griping her way around, I began looking forward to wheeling around town with my four kids in tow. Given a chance, the kids opened up. We laughed together, debated, questioned, shared our feelings and grew much closer. I still drive two hundred miles a week, but I look forward to every mile, because driving time has become family time in our car. Prime time, and time for giving. Cheerfully.

LOVE WITHOUT SMOTHERING

by Danny Kaye

The famous song and dance man gives some advice of his own.

Have you ever, as a parent, felt guilty about your children? Have you ever worried for fear you weren't giving them enough time, enough love, enough of yourself? If you have, and you're an unusual parent if you haven't, I'd like to pass along something I learned some years ago when our daughter, Dena, was quite small.

Dena is an only child and, like most very young children, she could never understand why occasionally her parents had to leave her. My work required me to travel a lot, but this is hard to explain to a three-year-old. Dena just didn't understand why I had to go away.

When she was about six, I used to fumble around, trying to prepare her for my departure so she wouldn't be quite so hurt when I did leave. I would be extra nice, or talk about plans for all kinds of new fun. Whenever I did such things, Dena would say, 'You're going away again, aren't you?'

And each time I returned home I rushed to her, and overwhelmed her with kisses and presents and promises of picnics and parties. All expressions of the guilt I felt at leaving her. I wanted her to overwhelm me too, and make up in one burst of love all that had accumulated during our separation.

I wanted very much to hear her say, 'I missed you'. But she never said it. Each time I left and each time I returned, I sensed a greater withdrawal by Dena.

While I was struggling to find some answer to this dilemma, I had to go off on a long trip.

The World Health Organization and the United Nations Children's Fund had told me that millions of children in Asia and Africa could be saved by modern medicine from the scourges of TB, leprosy, malaria, malnutrition, and the like, if the world could be made aware of their plight. They asked me to help make the world aware of them by visiting the WHO's centres to make a film called *Assignment Children*. I couldn't refuse.

At one point on the trip, I found myself in a hospital in New Delhi, India, in a room where a mother and father sat quietly watching their little son who had just been brought in from the operating room.

When the boy awoke I expected them to rush towards him. They continued to sit quietly in their corner. The boy looked around and saw them, but said nothing. After a while he called to them, and they came. They touched him gently, never losing the restraint they had on themselves, never showing any fear or concern, though they must have felt both deeply.

They attended to his need, and when done returned to sit quietly. When he wanted something they saw to it. The boy determined when he needed them and how much he needed them. The parents did not smother him with their love or their fears but they were pillars of strength and comfort and security.

The lesson was vividly in my mind and heart when I returned home, and Dena and her mother met me at the airport. This time I didn't bring the usual ton of gifts, nor did I lavish on Dena kisses and promises.

I greeted them both with a warm hug and kiss, and on the way home talked easily and casually about ordinary things. My wife, Sylvia, sensed what I was trying to do and, bless her, helped right along. I let Dena set the pace and ask the questions.

For once I was trying to find out what she wanted, not satisfy what I wanted.

When we got home Dena squeezed my hand and said what I had wanted to hear her say for a long time, 'I missed you, Daddy.'

I learned a lot that day – that day and the day I spent in a New Delhi hospital room watching a mother and father who knew how to give love, not smother it.

DON'T GIVE UP

by Marjorie Holmes

*It was a day to remember, a day that was to demand almost
super-human speed, strength and endurance.*

Whenever I am asked, as frequently as I am, what single quality a
parent needs most, I immediately answer, 'Endurance'.

Not faith or patience or even love, vital though they are, but
sheer physical and emotional endurance. The ability to make it
through another night, another day. Through those times when
conflicts, complications, problems swoop down upon a family like
a flock of clamouring birds demanding help, comfort and instant
solutions.

When there doesn't seem to be enough of you to go around,
but there is. When it seems you'll surely collapse, but you don't.
Days when the sheer number and nature of the difficulties become
funny. Or weeks, sometimes months, when sickness and troubles
strike in sequence like a soap opera, another dire episode beginning just as the last crisis is being resolved.

My journal records the highlights of a typical day so hectic that
a woman or man, can only pray, 'Hold me up a little longer Lord!'

No school today. Planned to sleep late then plant flowers.
Phone rang at dawn, kid who wanted to buy Mark's car said
to meet him right away at bowling alley. Told Mark I'd follow
and bring him back. Lost Mark at traffic lights, couldn't find
the bowling alley. Finally got there, Mark had phoned, his car

for sale had broken down. Called his dad to come and get
him. Mark distraught. Arrived home to discover a big mess in
kitchen and the cake Melanie was baking to surprise a sick
friend burning while she giggled on the phone. Cake ruined.
Melanie distraught. Upstairs, Mickie in throes of making a
new dress for big date. Sewing machine snarling up. Dad,
who can fix it, still off trying to fix Mark's car. Mickie distraught. I find oilcan and by some miracle fix it, but get oil on
dress. Mickie tries on dress and howls, 'It looks awful!' Oil
won't come out, dress doesn't fit. Both of us distraught. Mal
bursts in to remind me his Scout uniform has to be done up
and patches sewn on for parade at three o'clock. He rushed
off with pals for ball game in yard and breaks window. Dog
throws up. I wash, iron, sew, bake and try to patch up cake,
dress, window, dog and people until dark. Flowers didn't get
planted but they will. Everybody happy tonight, everybody
survived. W.e do somehow.

I do find that God sees us through such days. He not only holds
us up, he gives us an extra burst of strength, and sometimes at the
very moment we think we'll go to pieces, like that window. I vividly
remember that was my own moment of near-explosion – when that
ball came crashing into the house, I opened my mouth to scream,
but instead began to laugh. Suddenly the whole day seemed like a
comedy, exasperating, but challenging my performance and inge-
nuity as a woman. I felt suddenly renewed in energy and spirit,
ready to cope with whatever came next. God even fortifies us with
a sense of humour that gives us a second wind.

There are other times more serious. Years ago, when I was expecting a third child and the older two were small, I nursed them
alone through a series of illnesses, even as I struggled to finish writing a novel. It was during World War II; we had moved to a strange
city, and my husband was away. First measles, then mumps. Then
only two days after Mickie was back in school and I was back at
the typewriter, her little brother climbed fretfully on my lap. I was

so tired and frustrated that I tried to put him down before realizing, with a start of fear, that once more his little body was hot. I opened his shirt to examine his chest. Again he was covered in a rash. Wearily I trudged to the phone to tell the doctor, 'The measles must have come back.'

'Are you sure? I'll be right over.' She was a fine woman, who made house calls in emergencies. 'I'm afraid it's worse than that,' she said, putting away her stethoscope. 'It looks like scarlet fever. You'll have to be quarantined.'

Mickie raced in, elated at all that was happening at school. She struggled not to cry when I told her. 'I won't get it Mummy,' she promised bravely. 'I'll help you.' But she did get it, and was a very sick little girl. Night after night I changed sweat-soaked sheets, bathed burning foreheads, held spoons of medicine and cups of water to parched lips. Day after day I rocked and sang and cut paper dolls and read stories. And when they napped and I should have been napping, I went to bed with a portable on my knees and pecked out a few more paragraphs.

Did the quarantine last three weeks or three years? It seemed an eternity. Scarlet fever was considered so contagious then, nobody could come near us. Not even help, if we could have found it. Not even my husband, if he'd been in the city. We kept in touch by phone and it was arranged that he come home the minute the quarantine was lifted.

At last the day came when the yellow warning was peeled from the doorway. We were out of prison! And their father would be home that night.

'We won't fumigate,' Dr Bates said. 'But you'll have to go over every inch of the upstairs with disinfectant and burn everything burnable, and of course wash and air the bedding. The children must be bathed and shampooed and put out in the sun while you're doing it. And by all means, work in a nap for yourself if you can. You'll need it.'

My head whirled, but I felt fired with joyous new confidence and strength. I wanted everything sparkling anyway for my husband's homecoming. But it was a day to remember, a day that was to demand almost super-human speed, strength and endurance.

Running up and downstairs with disinfectant and shampoo and towels. Into the basement to start the washing in a small lingerie machine never meant for sheets; they had to be wrung out by hand. Into the garden to struggle with a clothesline that didn't want to stay up, then start hanging things out – away from the smoke of the fire where the children were forlornly saying goodbye to the books and toys and teddy bears that had comforted them in their misery. Their wet heads made them look like just-hatched birds, especially in the skimpy faded garments I'd dug out for them to wear until the contents of their bureaux could be sunned on a balcony. I thanked God for that balcony, for it was close to the bedrooms. I had to drag the mattresses only down a hallway to reach it for their airing and sunning.

The children had to be watched; they were so excited to be out they were racing about and I was afraid of a relapse. When the little boy climbed the fence and ran down the street, I spanked him when I caught him. Then we both cried, hugging each other on the steps. The breakfast plates still faced us when we all came in for lunch at three o'clock – with the scrubbing of woodwork and floors, and windows not even begun.

And it was about that time that a little song began in my heart. 'Hold me up a little longer, Lord.' And he did. Like the miracle of the loaves and fishes, time and strength were provided. By five o'clock the last of the washing was on the line. By six the stripped house smelled like a hospital, but was shining. By 6.30 the fresh, fragrant sheets were back on the beds with Mickie helping. By 7.30 the children and I were fed and dressed and watching out of the window. And tired, bone-tired, but filled with a marvellous sense of triumph at all that had been accomplished, I was shakily putting on lipstick and listening for the sound of a taxi in the driveway.

When my husband came in, exclaiming at how great we all looked, I collapsed in his arms. The Lord had held me up as long as he needed to. God gives us the endurance to survive these trials with children, and to survive the deeper, more complex emotional trials, which almost no family is spared. Perhaps the physical ones are just rehearsals for the impending larger crises we will be called upon to face, and surmount: Quarrels. Temptations. Stormy romances. Problems concerning jobs or college or sometimes even the law. Disappointments far more significant than a ruined cake or car or dress. Healings that can't be achieved just by carrying medicine to a feverish child. Protection that can't be provided by simply scrubbing down a house.

But this I know: Whatever life asks us to face, we need not be afraid. God will see us through it, hold us up as long as we need him. I knew it then; I know it now.

JOE GOES TO DISNEYLAND

by Lois Woods

Kids stuff? He was only eighty-eight years old.

Take Pops along on our holiday?

'I'd like to invite your dad,' my husband, Bob, said. 'But would he be able to keep up?'

I sighed. We were planning our summer holidays, and we'd just learned that the Bunker family – my father's family – was holding its seventy-fourth annual reunion. The Bunkers trace their ancestry back to the early 1600s, and every year family members come from far and wide to swap stories, show off pictures of offspring, and get acquainted and updated generally.

Pops had been to one of these family reunions about five years ago and he'd always talked about going again. But at the age of eighty-eight, he had a left knee that sometimes buckled unexpectedly, so he walked with a cane.

'Pops would have too much trouble keeping up,' I said. 'And the trip would be hectic and exhausting. He'd never want to join us.' But we called him up to ask anyway.

'Can't wait!' Pops said excitedly. 'I'll get packing right away.'

We live in western Washington, and Pops's home is about 150 miles northwest of us in a little logging town called Forks, where he makes cedar chests, burl clocks and wind whirls, and sells them. Now I'd have to make arrangements to get Pops down to our home in Summer.

'Guess we'll have to drive up and get him,' I sighed.

I called Pops to let him know we'd be up to get him. 'No,' Pops said. 'I'll drive myself or stay home. Besides, I want to visit my nieces on the way down.'

A few days later – *beep, beep*. Who was in the driveway?

Pops emerged from his small blue pickup, all waves and smiles. 'When do we hit the road for California?' he asked. 'This trip is going to be great.'

I'd squeezed every extra penny I could manage out of our budget to cover the extra expense of the trip. *It will be tight,* I thought ruefully, gazing into my wallet. But then Pops pulled out *his* wallet and flashed his traveller's cheques.

'I've got six hundred dollars,' he announced, 'and some cash besides. I'm paying for my own room and tickets.'

'Okay, Pops.'

'And my share of petrol and meals.'

We flew into Sacramento, rented a car and drove to my nephew's home in nearby Woodland.

Along the way we saw rice paddies and fields of sunflowers. While we were in Woodland, my niece travelled down with her three children.

There were non-stop reminiscences and a lot of brand-new hugs and stories.

As we continued on out of town, I glanced sympathetically at Pops. If I was worn out from all the visiting, he must be too.

'I've seen two of my grandchildren and five of my great-grandchildren,' he exulted. 'This is the greatest trip I've ever had!'

'Yes, Pops,' I agreed. As I dropped my head against Bob's shoulder in exhaustion, I heard the rustle of the map in the backseat as Pops eagerly checked out our next stop.

We drove south where we visited my Aunt Esther. She's an elegant, stately woman of eighty-three, and when we left, she filled our suitcases with her homemade apricot jam and shelled walnuts from her own trees. A minute after we'd waved goodbye, Pops was munching nuts and checking guidebooks. 'This Solvang sounds real interesting,' he said.

Solvang is a Danish community thirty-five miles north of Santa Barbara, and its sunny streets bustled with activity. 'You kids explore all you want,' Pops said. 'I'll sit here in the shade under this tree. Don't worry about me.'

But worry comes naturally to me. As Bob and I browsed through the shops, I thought of Pops, leaning on his cane, bored. Alone.

'We've got to get back to him,' I said, tugging at my husband's sleeve.

There was the tree – but where was Pops? He was laughing and talking to a young couple and their children.

When we got back in the car, Pops pulled a small package from his pocket. 'Got you a present,' he said. I looked at the beautiful uncut crystal, twisted gracefully on a delicate silver chain, and knew it had cost more than he could afford. I swallowed hard. 'Thank you, Pops,' I managed.

We pulled into Anaheim and checked into a hotel just blocks from Disneyland. There were Bunkers, Bunkers everywhere, some fifty strong, of all ages and from all over the country. A tall, debonair man looked at my name tag, and his face lit up. 'Is your father here?' he asked eagerly. 'I've been writing to him for years but we've never met.' It was Frank Bunker, a distant cousin. He and Pops were both the sons of farmers in the Northwest Territory. I hailed Pops over, and the two retreated to a corner and started recalling the changes they'd seen in their lifetimes.

Every time I looked over, more family members were gathered around them, marvelling and laughing at their stories of the first electricity and indoor plumbing, the first telephones, aeroplanes and motorcars.

The planners of the reunion had scheduled lots of free time so the Bunkers could visit Disneyland. We went, of course, and Pops reluctantly agreed to be scooted from ride to ride in a Disneyland wheelchair. 'But I don't want to slow you down,' he said.

We joined one of the long lines that snaked back and forth and back again, and prepared to inch our way slowly to the Jungle Cruise. The attendants spotted us with Pops in his wheelchair. 'Go around there,' they said, pointing to the exit. 'They'll put you right on.'

The Jungle Ride. The Enchanted Tiki Room. Pirates of the Caribbean. We were directed into more exits – right to the front of the line – than most people ever *leave* from. 'Pops, you've got us into twice as many rides as we'd have been able to take by ourselves,' I said.

Pops wasn't listening. He was eyeing the Big Thunder Mountain Railroad, where cars shot over an undulating track while shrieking riders held on for dear life. 'That looks like fun,' Pops said.

As we disembarked from the Thunder Mountain coaster, Bob and I clutched each other. Was Pops okay?

'Look,' he said, 'it's Minnie Mouse.'

Back in the hospitality suite with the Bunker Family Associates, talk turned to the diamond-anniversary meeting, the seventy-fifth, coming up the following year. It would be held at the other side of the country.

'I'll start saving right away,' Pops said. 'I have to go to that one.'

The reunion ended with Sunday brunch, and on the way out of town we accepted an invitation from one of Pops's nieces to visit her son's church in Los Angeles. The sermon was given by my second cousin. I looked over at Pops, his face shining once again with curiosity and eagerness.

After the service, other worshippers crowded around. 'I'm so happy you could join us,' the minister said. 'Your father's enthusiasm does us all good.'

Enthusiasm. The word is from the Greek *en theos,* from God. A God-given excitement, a spirit-filled zeal.

For new experiences.

For loved ones.

For life.

This June Pops is planning to go to that family reunion in New Hampshire. We've got the plane tickets, and in spite of a year that included some health problems, he says he's going no matter what.

At eighty-nine he'll still be the life of the party.

Me, I'm catching Pops's enthusiasm just thinking about it.

THE CASE OF THE LONGHAIRED SON

by Phyllis Malone

I have learned not only about dealing with a teenager but also about how to keep a marriage intact while the flak whistles round you.

My husband and I had had minor disagreements over raising the children, as I suppose all couples do, but never one that divided us like the issue of Dru's long hair.

Frank, being a retired Air Force officer, wanted a spit-and-polish crew cut look in his only son. Dru argued that all the other kids had long hair. And I, dreading a clash between them, tried to make light of the problem.

'What harm does it really do?' I urged Frank. 'You know how important it is at his age to be part of the crowd.'

'Long hair on a fifteen-year-old boy, especially curly hair, makes him look like a girl,' Frank retorted.

But in the end – with my backing – Dru got his way. And if I hoped the hair would satisfy his need to conform, I was mistaken.

At first, there were those dreadful records that make you want to buy earplugs, not to mention their lyrics. He and his friends all began wearing untidy clothes, which seemed to be accessories to their Samson-style hairdos.

Of course, there's nothing new in this situation. Family after family has been through it or is going through it. But my husband

and I have learned some things that might be helpful to other couples, not only about dealing with a difficult six-foot-two teenager but also about how to keep a marriage intact while the flak whistles all around you.

With some boys, I'm sure, the long hair is just a stage. The exterior appearance may be sloppy, but it doesn't corrode the inner person. Grades, personal habits, morals remain undamaged. But when Dru began getting D's at school, I knew with a sinking feeling that we were in for serious difficulties.

'Why all the commotion?' Dru asked calmly. '*D* is a pass. Don't sweat it.'

'D is far below what you are capable of doing, and you know it,' I answered hotly.

For that was just the trouble – we *were* sweating it, Frank and I, and most of the heat seemed to rise between the two of us. Frank blamed me for being too permissive. In turn I accused him of applying military standards of performance and obedience to his family.

One wintry Saturday afternoon Dru came home and said calmly, 'I skidded into another car, but no damage done. Just a few scratches.'

'You'll have to talk it over with Dad,' I said. 'He'll be upset, but he will be understanding if you just tell him the whole truth and keep your temper.'

I couldn't have been more wrong. Dru went into the garage where Frank was working and the shouting on both sides began immediately. Frank couldn't see why Dru hadn't been a more careful driver, and his son refused to understand why his dad was so excited over a few scratches on the car.

'I can't please anybody around here,' Dru shouted, then stormed from the house to be gone the rest of the day and night. I headed for the garage.

'Why did it have to be a shouting contest?' I demanded of my husband. 'He told you the truth. I had told Dru you would understand, and you made a liar out of me. You wouldn't talk to your friends like that.'

'I don't pay insurance bills on my friends cars either,' he snapped back at me.

What was happening to us? During Frank's years in the Air Force, periods of lonely separations had taught us to treasure our time together. Now here we were either snarling at each other or hardly speaking at all.

I felt miserable. Up to this point I thought that somehow things would work out because I had been storming the gates of heaven with my prayers that Dru would straighten out.

Aware that there must be something wrong with my method of praying, I began searching the Bible for an answer. In James I found it. 'But if any of you lacks wisdom, he should pray to God, who will give it to him . . .'

This was it. I had been urging God to change my son instead of asking God for his wisdom on the problem. Once I became willing to seek God's help, the next step was to be willing to seek outside help for the whole family. I first went to our minister, and he referred me to a specialist in family counselling. It took several more months before I could overcome the block of pride and call for an appointment. When I told my husband what I'd done, I braced myself for his disapproval. I was wrong again. Frank was also ready for outside help.

During those once-a-week counselling sessions, we learned some things about our family – things we might have seen for ourselves if we had been more willing to look at our failings and talk them out.

Frank and I were both surprised to learn that we had been playing a you-win-this-time, I-win-next game when it came to decisions about the children, rather than trying to arrive at mutually accepted compromises. By failing to agree, we had presented to Dru and our daughters a divided front. And that poor situation had been aggravated by Frank's absences from home. Even his present civilian job as an aircraft-accident investigator often took him away from home, and Dru especially had learned to appeal to me alone at such times.

Now, with the encouragement of the counsellor, Frank and I sat down together to go over the whole list of rules for our children, to be in effect no matter who was consulted: study hours, chores, bedtimes, punishments, television. It took us several hours, and we both had to make certain concessions to our convictions, but in the process I found myself drawing closer to my husband.

The day that Frank and I announced to Dru and our girls, Laurie and Shannon, that we had agreed on certain rules and procedures for them, there was some spoken resistance. Yet I sensed they too had a feeling of inner relief that their parents were united and that they knew now exactly where they stood.

As the counsellor gently probed into the roles Frank and I played in the home, I saw areas where I had taken on too much authority. Too often I had come between my husband and son, trying to be a peacemaker. Perhaps Frank's frequent absences had made me try to be both father and mother in our home, and formed too close a bond between Dru and me. I saw that I needed to re-examine my role as a woman, and to let the all-important relationship between father and son develop without my complicating presence.

While a lot of new understanding has come to me through these counselling sessions, my ability to accept and to change has resulted through the power of prayer. The verse in James opened my eyes to how much I was depending on my own power and how little on his. The result was an insensitive mother and an unappreciative wife.

Prayer now helps me keep things in perspective. I see now that parents can fail with a child, but that no failure needs be permanent. Teenagers are going to make mistakes, and thus they can learn about themselves and become individuals in their own right. Yet we parents tend to resist letting this happen because we think our child's imperfections reflect upon us and spotlight our own weaknesses. Frank and I have been able to conclude that since it isn't fair for us as parents to take all the credit for our children's successes, we shouldn't feel guilty for all their failures either.

Above all, prayer has helped recapture God's view of marriage, as I glimpsed it on our wedding day. It was Frank I promised God to love and to cherish then, before we knew if there'd be children or not, and I know now that he must continue to come first.

There are still upsets in our home. Dru still has his long hair; there are occasional flare-ups between him and his dad; Frank and I still have our disagreements, as any two people must. But there is a great difference now. My husband and I have re-established at the centre of our home the relationship between the two of us from which all other right family relationships flow.

Friction with a teenaged child, after all, is a forecast of the day when he will be setting up a life and home of his own. One of the greatest gifts we can give Dru now is the example of our own happy marriage. It also means that Frank and I must start preparing for the day when our family will be again, as it began, two whom God has joined together.

FAMILIES CAN BE BETTER

by Margaret Peale

Probably the hardest thing for parents to do is to let their children go.

The hardest job in the world, I think, is being a parent. Looking back over my own family life, I often wonder at my parents' patience, understanding, and wisdom. Each of us three children, probably, can find some lack in our family life for which we will have to compensate in other ways.

Parents cannot hope to raise perfect families, but I believe the job of parenthood is to help children develop their personalities in such ways that they in turn will make even better parents.

I believe that a good family life is dependent on the family's growing together. Mum and Dad always made us feel that the things that were important to us were also important to them. My two main interests in high school were basketball and singing. An important game would never go by without one or both of my parents there watching me. I never asked them to come, but they knew how much it meant to me and would always fit it into their busy schedules.

Because our parents like whomever we like, a constant stream of friends parades in and out of the house. One day the door to our apartment opened and John, my brother, stood on the threshold with seven other boys.

'I've brought some friends to stay the night. Mum. That's okay, isn't it?'

147

Without batting an eyelash, Mother smiled and said, 'Why, of course, come in.' At that moment she wasn't sure she had extra beds, but John knew she would provide.

Mum and Dad indoctrinated us early with the idea that each member of the family has an equal share in family responsibilities, and that we are a team of five.

Out of this atmosphere grew a feeling of trust. We never had any strict rules of do's and don'ts. We discussed what was right, wrong and sensible and then Mum and Dad trusted us to use our own judgment and act accordingly.

Into this atmosphere of family discussion God was brought as a necessary and vital factor. Religion was thus never really taught us; it was just practiced. Perhaps that fact accounted for the lack of rebellion that so many ministers' children go through.

An example of how this combination of family closeness and faith works came at the end of my junior year in college. I was asked to be an advisor to thirty new girls during my final year. This required living with the girls, and actually being part of their adjustment to life in a new college. I shied away from the job, actually refusing it once, because I felt I couldn't handle the responsibilities it entailed. Then I called my parents.

Dad said, 'God has given you this chance for a purpose. If you stand still and never take advantage of your opportunities, you won't get anywhere in life. Have the courage to accept the position and God will make known to you the reasons behind it.'

I did as he advised, and it proved to be the most meaningful experience of my college career.

Once, when John and Elizabeth and I were quite young, our favourite pastime was throwing water bombs, sand bombs and paper aeroplanes out of our apartment window.

While I am sure it caused Mum and Dad some moments of acute embarrassment, this passing fad was handled with real understanding. We were always punished, usually by cleaning up the mess or by apologizing to the caretaker, but never forbidden to see our friends. Again, a sensible and adult discussion of our actions turned the trick.

Probably the most difficult thing for Mother to face was the time John and I decided we didn't want to go to church any more. This was particularly drastic for a minister's family, but careful searching uncovered the real reason – we didn't want to walk down the aisle and sit in the pastor's pew.

In spite of Mother's desire to have the family sit together in church, she said, 'You can sit wherever you like.' So, for years, we sat in the front row of the balcony – the most conspicuous place in the church, I might add – but we went to church.

Probably the hardest thing for parents to do is to let their children go, but it is one of the most important. Recently, when a girl friend and I moved into an apartment of our own, I discovered something: If parents have created a home filled with love, under-standing and trust, and have helped each child develop his own personality and make his own decisions, parents need never fear losing their children.

ALONE THROUGH THE DARK

by Ruth Hagen

The fearsome scale of the mountains couldn't break the spirit of three generations.

I was visiting family in August 1987 when my daughter Judy, and eighteen-year-old granddaughter, Marcy, suggested we drive up to their rustic cabin in the foothills above California's San Antoine Valley. Off we went, zigzagging thirty-six miles up and down mountain roads for the better part of the afternoon. For the last few miles the road was mostly one lane, so steep and narrow that I worried Judy's four-wheel-drive wouldn't make it. The road was a mix of powdery dirt and brittle pieces of shale on which the Bronco lurched and slid terrifyingly close to the edge of the rocky cliff.

As soon as we arrived and got inside the cabin, Judy remarked with a grin that she had some good news. 'The mice didn't chew through the telephone cord,' she said. 'And they didn't even eat our phone book.' She held up the one-page sheet of local numbers, mostly those of ranchers, with no more than a dozen listings. The three of us had a chuckle as we unpacked our provisions.

The crisp mountain air gave me a good appetite, and I enjoyed Judy's supper of potatoes, sausage and peach cobbler. After we cleared the dinner dishes Marcy announced, 'Mum, the water tank is pretty low so I'll take the Bronco down to the pump.'

All the water used in the cabin had to be hauled from down below, where there was a natural spring with a pump beside it.

I was nervous about Marcy driving that narrow dirt road so close to dark. But Judy reminded me my independent granddaughter had driven those mountain roads many times. 'Remember, you've only got eight or ten inches of clearance in places,' she warned as Marcy left. 'Since we've had a dry spell, the roadbed is really shaky. Make sure you hug the side of the mountain.'

As Marcy drove off I said a quick prayer. Judy watched her daughter's progress from the cabin's picture window, through which you could see the narrow road wind its way down the mountain.

Maybe fifteen minutes passed when suddenly Judy screamed, 'Oh, no! Dear God, help us!'

The cabin door slammed. Judy had taken off running. As quick as I could, I followed. 'Judy, wait!'

'The Bronco went over the cliff, Mum! Come on, we have to help Marcy!'

At seventy-eight, I couldn't run as fast as Judy. She was out of sight after the first turn in the road. I ran on and on, down the hill, up the next, at least a quarter of a mile, trying to catch up. In the gathering darkness, it was getting hard to see anything ahead of me. Where had Judy gone? *God, please help me know what to do.*

Something made me stop in my tracks. I strained to see a sign of movement. There was only silence.

'Judy where are you?' I screamed into the gathering darkness.

Down the cliff to my right I heard a frantic warning: 'I'm down here, Mother! Don't come near the edge! I slipped on loose rocks and fell over. I'm down maybe seventy feet.'

'Judy, what can I do?'

'Just stay back, Mum! The road is giving out all over! I think I can crawl back up. I saw the Bronco's roof as I was falling and heard Marcy calling for help. She's alive, Mum! But she's way down in the ravine. Go back to the cabin and phone for help. Tell them to send a helicopter. We've got to get Marcy out!'

I wanted to look over and make sure Judy was really okay but I knew I might fall too, so I turned and started running back up the hill I had just tumbled down. By then I was exhausted and almost weak with panic. My heart was pounding and I was gasping. I stumbled and landed hard on my face. I tried to get up but couldn't.

I started to sob. 'Dear God, please give me the strength to get back to the cabin so I can call for help.'

It's hard to describe what happened then. One moment I was helpless on the ground, the next moment an electric current seemed to surge through me. I heard the words *I am here*. They were as clear as if the speaker were next to me.

I got to my feet without a wobble. When I stood, I felt relaxed and rested. A surge of pain-free energy propelled me forward. Confidently, I started to run, faster than I had before. When I reached the cabin I hurtled through the front door and called the operator.

As I sputtered out the details of the accident, I realized I had no idea where I was. The cabin had no address, and I didn't know which roads led to it. In my panic I hadn't thought to ask Judy for those details. I remembered we had gone through a cattle range, but the landmarks I described to the operator only confused her. I told her to stand by and hung up. I had to get Judy to the phone so she could give directions.

I grabbed a torch and a walking stick. I dashed back toward Judy but abruptly came to a fork in the road I didn't remember. Which way to go? 'Lord, help me!'

Again a sense of calmness, then a reassuring certainty. *That way.* I continued to run with energy and determination. Up the hill, down the hill, up the second hill. In the shrouding darkness, I was unsure of where my loved ones were. Suddenly I sensed the right place to pause. 'Marcy! Judy!' I shouted.

A faint voice filtered up from the rocks and spiky bushes below. I heard, 'I'm here, Grandma.' Another voice: 'Mum!' It was Judy once again; I had stopped at the exact site of the accident.

Thank you, Lord.

I dropped to my knees and lay flat to inch myself to the cliff's brink. Holding the walking stick over the edge, I asked Judy if she could see it was there.

'I'm coming, Mum. I'm almost there. I'm really scratched up.'

I could hear gravel cascading away from where Judy was trying to climb. Minutes later I felt her grab the end of the stick. I heaved with all my strength, never imagining I could pull up my daughter but I did.

Judy crawled onto my lap, shaking and sweating, and immediately passed out. I held her close and stroked her forehead. 'Judy, wake up. We have to get help for Marcy! Judy wake up!' I kept talking and rubbing her head. Finally some minutes later, she came to. I pulled her to her feet and we started walking. Dazed and bleeding, Judy fell three times as we went back to the cabin.

There, we heard the phone ringing. It was the rescue team. Judy gave them directions and we started back down the mountain to Marcy. I held on to Judy, not for my sake but for hers. She was weak, bruised and bleeding. But I was still strong enough to support her.

A half hour later fire trucks arrived, and paramedics came by helicopter. It took four hours to free Marcy from the wreckage at the bottom of the cliff. At last the local sheriff was able to pull her out the rear end of the Bronco and carry her on his back to the waiting helicopter.

Marcy was treated for a broken leg, crushed ankle, broken foot and fractured finger. The next day the sheriff came to visit her in the hospital and said, 'The mountain didn't beat you. You'll be back.'

No, the mountain hadn't beaten us. My granddaughter, daughter and I all have our lives to prove it.

TEEN FOR A DAY

by Karen Barber

Wacky Tuesday gave Mum the chance to see what it was like being a teenager again.

We had just moved and I had to drop off my son Chris at his school. I was ready to leave, but he wasn't. Chris's brown hair flopped across his forehead as he jerked away in annoyance.

'Mum, we're leaving too early. You just don't understand!'

Tension crept into my neck. Now that Chris was a teenager, at times I felt like I was attempting to communicate with a being from another planet and not with the fun-loving offspring I had been raising for the past 15 years. 'What is there to understand?' I shot back. 'In case there's traffic we need to leave at 7.45.'

'I can't hang around all by myself before the bell,' Chris mumbled.

'We're not risking being late for such a ridiculous reason,' I answered. We left promptly at 7.45 a.m.

The following week Chris staggered in from school and dumped his backpack with a thump that made me frown. When I asked him about his classes, it became clear he hadn't been participating in class discussions, 'Chris,' I argued, 'you have good ideas.'

'But none of the other kids say anything.'

So what? I wrinkled my forehead. Maybe I was the one who just wasn't getting it. *Why won't a smart kid speak up in class?*

That weekend I overheard Chris telling his brother he had kicked someone at school. 'Chris!' I horned in. 'How could you do such a thing?'

154

'You don't know how crowded it is,' he protested. 'The guy was in my way and he was just standing there talking to somebody.'

'Don't ever do that again!' I scolded. Chris turned and stomped off to his room. As his stereo blasted I prayed, *Lord, what does it take to understand a teenager?*

The first week in October I received a notice about the school's 'Wacky Tuesday'. Parents were invited to attend school in place of their teenagers and the teenagers were to go to their parents' place of work. There were rules: Each parent had to stay for the entire day and take notes for his or her child. Apparently, several dozen parents did it every year. It sounded interesting, so I signed up.

The day before Wacky Tuesday I told Chris, 'This afternoon when I pick you up I want you to show me how to find all your classes.'

'No way, Mum. Nobody showed me around the first day. I want you to know exactly how I felt.'

'Fine,' I answered, thinking. *What on earth has got into him?*

On Wacky Tuesday, Chris put on a shirt and a tie and went to the office with my husband, Gordon. I pulled on a turtleneck, slacks and running shoes. I heaved a backpack crammed with Chris's books over my shoulders and was off to school at a quarter to eight.

Inside the school with time to spare and no one to talk to, I stood uncomfortably, listing under the weight of the backpack.

Okay I'd try to make sense of the map the school had given out. I had to get to room 5109, placed for some reason on the first level.

I plunged into a traffic jam of students, gym duffels, and open lockers and turned down the wrong hall. I raced to correct my course and found the stairway blocked by a girl with a gargantuan book bag. As the girl prattled mindlessly with some friends, I thought, *this kid is as effective a roadblock as a hippopotamus.* I elbowed my way through oncoming traffic, not bothering to say excuse me as I rushed.

In Algebra the teacher handed out a graded exam and went through the solutions on the blackboard. She wrote so fast I could barely copy the figures down. It was a scene from a nightmare: I walk into an exam and haven't the foggiest notion how to do anything.

The knot in my stomach tightened during second and third periods. In Geography the kids working on our project responded to my suggestions with blank stares. In IT Skills, the lesson was on keys I rarely used.

Lunch was next. There were several empty places, but I hesitated. *What if they're saving those places for their friends? Or don't want me around?* Finally I spotted a bunch of parents and practically sprinted to an empty spot at their table.

I had been looking forward to English, and had eagerly read the assigned pages in *Lord of the Flies*. The teacher asked the class how they envisioned the forest fire the boys carelessly start. *Such details don't matter; the book is more of a parable than a news account,* I wanted to say. For some reason my hand stayed firmly by my side.

Maybe the teacher is about to make that point and I would steal her thunder. Or maybe I'll sound like a show-off and the others will laugh at me.

Biology was my last class, and it was lab day. We frantically measured and cut straws into various lengths to represent differing ionization rates. The final bell rang just when I read the rather odd last question on the lab sheet: 'What did you learn about yourself in this lab?'

I gathered my books and plunged into the frantic hall. *I'm not fighting those hippopotamuses through the crowded halls just to stash these in Chris's locker,* I decided. Instead, I fled out the nearest exit.

My car was parked three blocks away. By the second block the backpack straps cut into my shoulders and my lower back was screaming out that I was, after all, a middle-aged woman. When I walked through the kitchen door and threw down that book bag, I felt a thousand pounds lighter. *So this is how Chris feels when he gets home . . .*

Suddenly, I found myself mentally filling in that last question on the biology lab sheet. I had done everything I had been criticizing

Chris for. At lunch I had dreaded sitting with strangers. In English class I had kept quiet. And in my panic to get to class on time I had done some aggressive pushing.

When Chris got home from his dad's office he looked at his stuffed book bag and groaned. 'Don't tell me I have that much homework.'

'You don't,' I explained sheepishly. 'I didn't feel like fighting the hippopotamuses to get to your locker. High school's hard work. I'm glad I got to see what you have to deal with.'

'Yep.' Chris' nonchalant shrug could mean 'typical parent, stating the obvious again'. But I could see the shrug went along with a look in his eye that meant my fun-loving offspring was communicating, 'Well, Mum finally gets it'.

I grinned. Yes, I finally 'got' not just my teenager, but also what the book of Proverbs has been teaching parents for thousands of years: 'Be of an understanding heart.'

THE KNOCK AT MY DOOR

by Claudia Leaman

At first I didn't listen. Finally I did.

I could hardly believe what my older brother, Hal, was saying to me. His suggestion was ridiculous, absurd – he wanted me to get down on my knees and give my life to God! I was shocked and repelled. My brother had become a Jesus freak!

It was the last night of my weekend visit with him in Cambridge, where he was studying. We were sitting in his apartment, on the rollaway couch that served as my bed, discussing religion. He could not have chosen a touchier subject, for I had recently decided that I was an atheist. I was just eighteen and a few months earlier had started college, leaving home for the first time.

I tried to explain to Hal the way I felt. 'Ever since I can remember,' I told him, 'I've gone to church and Sunday school just because it was the thing to do. But now that I'm in college, I realize that I never thought any of it out for myself. I can't justify my old beliefs to myself or to the kids in the dorm. I think I've been an atheist all along.'

'Barb,' Hal said slowly, calling me by my family nickname, 'God is still there. All you have to do is ask him into your life.'

I had noticed in Hal a new kind of strength and assurance, and I admired that – but then I had always admired Hal. Ever since I was seven and my father died, Hal had been special to me, helping me with my lessons, giving me books to read. Now it seemed that if I couldn't trust Hal, there was no one I could trust.

Hal kept telling me what he thought I should do. Finally, just to please him, I did the last thing I ever pictured doing on a visit to my brother. I went down on my knees and repeated the words he suggested: 'God, please come into my life.' Nothing happened. I only felt awkward and embarrassed. After a short while I got up. Hal embraced me and said good night. I was grateful that he didn't ask me how I felt.

When he left the room I began to cry. I cried all night and most of the next day. Because I could no longer understand Hal. Because I was confused and alone.

The next time I saw my brother was a few months later at a family gathering. He made a point of talking to me alone. 'How do you feel about accepting God into your life?' he asked.

'It may be all right for you,' I blurted, 'but not for me.' Hal could see I didn't want to be questioned about it.

For ten years we dropped the subject, and I tried to put the experience out of my mind. During that time I graduated from college and began my acting career. I fell back into my old, half-understood ways of occasionally going to church. But I never quite knew why or what I was looking for there.

Early in 1977 I found myself in a rehearsal room with the director and cast of *Jesus Christ, Superstar.* I had a role as one of Jesus' followers, and we were preparing for a major production. Five months earlier I had played Sonya, also a follower of Christ, in *Godspell.*

When I got the role in *Superstar,* I promised myself that what had happened to me in *Godspell* wouldn't happen again. Acting in that play, in a local Pennsylvania production, had been one of the most frustrating experiences of my life. Night after night I saw something happen in the theatre that I had never seen before – an audience no longer made up of strangers, but of friends, singing and rejoicing together. But although I felt their exhilaration, I was unable to share it – the gospel narratives that the play is built around just didn't come alive for me.

Because acting was my whole world, I was willing to do anything to be a better actress – even if it meant going to the Bible to research my role. For the first time, I really read the gospels carefully. Now, waiting backstage at the theatre, I thought I was thoroughly prepared for the scene we were about to rehearse.

The director, an enthusiastic man, gave us our directions:

'Jesus has just been arrested. You run to the spot where he was taken away. You look everywhere for him, unable to believe what has happened. It's as though all your dreams have been shattered – everything you've loved and hoped for is gone.'

As I began to play the scene, I felt a tremendous sadness rise and clutch my throat. Deeply moved, I burst into tears and allowed them to pour down my face. Everyone thought I was only acting. Afterward another member of the cast came up to me and said, 'Claudia, that was great! How did you do it?'

'I don't know,' I told her. And I really didn't. It didn't occur to me that I was acting out my own deep feelings of loss, fear and loneliness, that the scene in the play was actually a scene from my life.

When the run of the play was over, I returned home to a routine that seemed even emptier and more aimless than before. I spent most nights in front of the television set wondering why my life had so little meaning.

One cold night in January, restless and unhappy, I opened the Bible. I came upon Revelation 3:20: 'Behold, I stand at the door, and knock: if any man hear my voice, and open the door, I will come in to him, and will sup with him, and he with me.' I began to think that Christ had been knocking at the door for a long time, at least since that long-ago night with Hal. Only God could know how to reach me through my desire to be a good actress, a desire that led me to the Bible and finally to him. Suddenly, an overwhelming surge of love and longing and gratitude flooded through me. Once again I went to my knees, this time thankfully welcoming God into my life. At last I knew that my life was complete, and that I was made whole.

About a year after playing in *Superstar* I saw Hal again at another family get-together. Over coffee, I told him about all the changes that had entered into my life along with Christ. 'For the

first time I really feel I know what's important. It's not as if everything has been all roses, but when something disappointing
happens – say I'm rejected for a part – I always have somewhere
to turn. I'm never completely alone any more.'

Hal was silent for a while. Then he said, 'Well, I'm not surprised.
I knew you were put in those two plays for a reason.'

We ended that evening with thanksgiving for God's hidden
guidance, for each other and for the role that moved from the stage
into my real life: a disciple of Christ.

5

WHEN HONESTY IS
THE BEST POLICY

*Honesty is the first chapter
of the book of wisdom.*

Thomas Jefferson

ADVENTURES OF A PEN PAL

by Myrtle Potter

Writing letters had been pure pleasure – until she started to pretend.

By the time I was in junior school I had fifteen pen pals with whom I corresponded faithfully. I found that being a pen pal was a non-threatening way of making friends. All my correspondents lived about fifteen miles away. They were all too young to drive, so the chances we'd meet were slim. Since I was extremely bashful, this suited me fine.

I found my correspondents in a local newspaper – its 'Junior Page' had a regular listing of young people looking for pen pals. I chose other girls' names, and before long I was receiving at least five letters a day and writing that many in return. I earned my stamp and stationery money by gardening and mowing lawns.

'What do you hope to accomplish with all this letter writing?' asked my uncle one day, eyeing the stack of mail I had received.

'I want to be a writer,' I said. 'I'm learning how.'

'Then you're going to have to see things from different points of view,' he said. 'All your letters are from girls. You should write to some boys. They look at life differently, you know.'

Hmmm, I thought, *my uncle has a point.* The next day I wrote to a boy named Norman. He wrote in reply, telling me he wanted to be a writer and horticulturist, travel and own a little house with a big garden. I loved to garden too. Our letters flew back and forth.

By this time I was in secondary school and my creative juices were just warming up. Apparently I could write well enough as a girl, but could I pass myself off writing as a boy? I tried a letter to another male name – but this time I signed my letter Myron. Soon 'Myron' had a lively correspondence going with other guys about camping, sports and Boy Scouts.

Once I had the boy stuff mastered, the next step was irresistible. I would pretend I was a boy and write to a girl! After choosing a feminine name from the newspaper's pen-pal list, I composed a letter in my most boy-like style. Using what I hoped was a manly flourish, I signed the name Mervin.

For months 'Mervin's' correspondence was mostly about school affairs, books and movies. And then one day I received a letter that shocked me. 'Mervin,' my girl pen pal wrote, 'you're the kind of boy I want to marry. In my dreams last night you kissed me! I'm coming to see you as soon as I can.'

I was horrified. I had never written anything even remotely romantic to this silly girl! I stopped my end of the correspondence immediately, but to my dismay she kept writing, insisting she was coming to visit. For the first time I realized that what I had done might hurt somebody.

One Sunday I was in the shower with my head covered with shampoo when Mum rapped on the door. 'Hurry out!' she called. 'One of your pen pals is here.'

I nearly fainted. It was probably that drippy girl wanting to kiss me. 'Lord,' I whispered, 'forgive me for letting that girl think I was a boy. Please help me.'

I made up my mind to stay in the bathroom until they left. But a few minutes later, Mum was at the door again. 'What's taking you so long? You're being very rude.'

'Mum, what's this visitor's name?'

'There are three of them. Your pen pal and two friends. I forget what they said their names were.'

'Are they girls?'

'No. Three boys.'

So it wasn't that lovesick girl. But I still could be in deep trouble. What if it was a boy expecting to find a boy?

'Mum, whom did my pen pal ask for when he came?'

'He asked for you, of course. Who do you think he came to see, Geronimo?'

I got dressed and was considering climbing out the window when someone started to play the funeral dirge on the piano below. The notes portrayed my feelings exactly. I knew then that whoever my pen pal was, he was shy and afraid too. Somehow that thought gave me courage.

I tiptoed toward the living room. 'Go on,' Mum hissed, and gave me a shove. I stumbled in, and the boys jumped up as if a firecracker had gone off. I must have looked a sight with my hair still glistening from my extended shower.

The four of us stood in tongue-tied silence until the boy closest to me stepped forward. 'I'm your pen pal,' he said. 'It's me, Norman.'

He was the one who wanted to be a writer and have a garden! 'How do you do?' I asked, greatly relieved.

Norman introduced his friends. 'I suppose I should have told you I was coming,' he said, looking so sheepish I felt sorry for him. He gestured toward the window. 'I got my driver's licence last week, so I borrowed my brother's car,' he said. 'Would you like to go for a ride?'

Mum had been listening behind the door. 'You can go,' she said. 'After the boys write their names, addresses and phone numbers in our guest book.'

I enjoyed the ride, but after Norman left, my fears came back. When Mum cornered me to ask what the fuss in the shower was all about, I knew it was time to confess. I told her about the girl in love with 'Mervin'.

She smiled. 'You've got yourself in quite a fix,' she said.

'I know,' I said. 'I feel awful about it.'

Mum's expression turned serious. 'I expect you do, Myrtle,' she said gently. 'That's what happens when we don't deal with others truthfully. You have to write to that girl, tell her you deceived her and ask for her forgiveness.'

I wrote that afternoon, and a few days later I received a wonderful letter back. 'I forgive you,' she wrote. 'It was my fault too. I've been seeing too many romantic movies.'

A few weeks later Norman took me for another ride; he found a much happier person. Soon he was visiting frequently. Knowing I could now relax and be myself, I got involved in school activities and gradually became too busy to write to any of my other pen pals. Consequently, they stopped writing – a cause for much jubilation on the part of my postman.

I learned several lessons from my pen-pal ventures. First, not to deceive anyone ever – it only brings unhappiness. I also learned the power of owning up when you do wrong, and the great relief forgiveness can bring. From then on I've never pretended to be someone I'm not. Believe me, it's made my life much more pleasant – and a lot less complicated.

Three years later Norman and I started college together, majoring in journalism and horticulture. After graduation he became garden editor of a popular magazine and I became garden editor of another. We got married, had two wonderful children and, eventually, three grandchildren who show a propensity for gardening and writing. It all turned out to be quite a postscript to my life as a pen pal!

TRUTH IS GOOD BUSINESS

by David Schwartz

Would you buy a car from this man?

For the past sixteen years I have bought and sold more than 3,000 used cars. And now I rent them. Through it all I believe I have learned the secret of business success. It's not really a secret, though I don't think enough people take advantage of it. Part of it lies in the fact that I am lazy. Let me explain how it all happened.

In 1968 I began working my way through university when a friend who was buying a new car offered to sell me his old one for the same price the dealer was allowing as a trade-in. I bought it, then resold it, making a £100 profit.

It seemed a good way to help defray college expenses, and from then on I bought and sold cars in this manner. By the time I graduated I found myself in the used-car business.

I began with a few old cars on a small space in the town. Here I really put into practice what I had learned in my college car dealings. If something was wrong with a car I was selling, I'd try to fix it. If I couldn't fix it, I would tell the prospective buyer up front. If the battery was weak, he'd know; if the car used a lot of oil, he wouldn't have to drive a hundred miles to find out.

'Dave, you're nuts,' argued a friend. 'Everybody knows you can't make any money in the used-car business that way.'

This is where my being lazy came in. The last thing I wanted was an angry customer charging back with fire in his eyes about some unexpected thing going wrong with his car. For me, this would be too much work and aggravation.

So if a fellow came into my shop and said, 'Look, I have £500 to spend on a car, what have you got?' I'd ask him what he needed.

'Oh, something with four doors.'

'Well, here's a 1965 Ford that runs pretty well. But after you drive it a hundred miles or so, the transmission will slip a little.'

He takes it out on a test drive, comes back and says, 'Okay, Dave, it's a deal.'

He leaves happy, and I'm happy. He knows what he's getting, and I have made a little profit. That's equitable, good news for everybody.

That first year I lost money, I really took a bath. But it wasn't my car-selling tactics. I hadn't yet learned how to judge people. Folks would give me money down on a car with a promise to pay.

Sometimes their word wasn't good enough. Eventually, I was able to tell the people I could trust and the ones I couldn't. I suppose you'd call that discernment.

My business began to grow. Satisfied customers told others, 'Hey, if you want a good deal on a used car, see Dave Schwartz.' Soon my little shop was jammed bumper to bumper with cars.

Then, through ignorance, I stepped into another good thing. The man across the street on Pico Boulevard was fighting a losing battle with his big garage and some store buildings. He had sunk himself too deep with other investments and owed his mother-in-law plus a third trustee on the property. He wanted someone to put down £2,000 and take over the payments. Again, wise business heads warned me, 'Dave, his overall asking price is way too much; the property isn't worth it.'

Well, I figured I could make the payments and I did need the space badly. All I needed was the down payment. And this is where I learned another lesson.

Basically, I'm a simple, informal guy who feels at home in blue jeans, a sweater, old tennis shoes and a jockey cap. However, when I went to the bank to borrow the down payment, I thought I'd improve my image. So I put on a three-piece suit, slicked down my hair and donned tight, shiny shoes. Well, during the interview with the bank manager, I felt as if I were suffocating. My hands were sweaty and I was restless. The banker sensed this, of course, and had absolutely no confidence in me.

A few weeks later, I went to another bank in my normal clothes – jeans, old shoes – feeling perfectly at home and confident. I got the loan.

I bought the property and moved my car business across the street, calling it 'Bundy Used Cars' because it was close to the better-known Bundy Street. Today, the property is worth many times what I paid for it.

More and more customers came in. Most of my cars were clunkers, but they all ran. Still, people would walk by and laugh, asking, 'How do you have the nerve to sell such homely cars?'

I scratched my head and thought. They were right. So I asked a sign painter to make a new sign: 'Bundy – Very Used Cars'.

Then something happened that changed the whole course of my business. A young woman walked in one morning carrying suitcases, 'You know,' she said, looking around wonderingly, 'ten different people told me to come here.'

I was amazed; I could never have paid for that kind of advertising. It turned out she had just graduated and had arrived in the town on a three-month work assignment. After looking over our stock, she bought a Corsair, 'as is', for £100.

That afternoon she phoned wanting to know if I knew of a good mechanic in her area.

'No,' I said. 'Why?'

'Well, my car broke down.'

'I'm sorry,' I said. 'I'll have it towed in. But come on over and I'll give you your money back.'

She almost dropped the phone.

Later on she found another car she liked. 'Look,' she suggested, 'instead of my buying it, how about renting it to me for the three months I'll need it? I'll be glad to pay you £150.'

'I'd like to,' I said, 'but I don't have the kind of insurance needed to rent cars.'

'Well,' she said thoughtfully, 'how about selling me the car for £150 so you can put it in my name. I'll assume responsibility for insurance and then in three months I'll return the car to you free and clear.'

I did some quick calculating. The car was really worth £200, but ... if she was going to bring it back ...

'Okay,' I said, 'you've got a deal.'

Three months later she drove up in the car, handed me the keys and kissed me. 'God bless you, Dave,' she said, 'that was the best deal I've ever had!'

She waved goodbye and as I stood there holding the keys, I reflected on what had happened. I had the car, the money and a customer who seemed to be very happy. A light bulb lit up in my head.

I went to some other local shops that were renting cars. Every owner warned me away from it. 'It's a can of worms, Dave, don't go near it.' Most of them were pulling out of it.

I spent the next several weeks asking them why it wouldn't work. From what they told me I began to learn what they were doing wrong. So I began my own operation: Bundy Rent-A-Used-Car.

I have to admit my cars looked, well, very used. But I believed that the worse a car looked, the better it should run. So maybe the '63 Austin had rusted fenders and a mismatched paint job, but we made sure everything mechanical was in apple-pie order before a customer drove it out.

But they sure looked awful. As one couple drove out in a 1969 Zephyr, I overheard the wife ask, 'Where's the ashtray?'

'Honey,' replied the husband, 'the whole car is an ashtray.'

A friend, Jeffrey Kramer, kidded me. 'Dave, your cars are so old that their radios only get the BBC Light Service!' He slapped his leg and laughed. 'You ought to call this place Rent-A-Wreck.'

Again that light bulb came on.

'I'll do it,' I said.

'Do what?' he asked.

'Just wait and see.'

I called my sign-painter friend, and that's how Rent-A-Wreck came into being.

There was a method in what my friend Jeffrey called my madness. I felt it steered away people who were too apprehensive, who would give me a lot of grief. I wanted only those who understood what they were getting, a car that was mechanically sound and safe but one that wouldn't necessarily bring admiring glances.

Even to this day I hesitate renting to someone that I feel is going to be a complainer, no matter how well he is treated. As I said, I'm basically lazy. I don't like to do anything over the second time. I'd rather take a little extra time at first to make sure it's done right. I believe every business transaction must be equitable, and that means people leaving with a smile, even if they're not customers. One would-be patron came into our office the other evening and after a few comments from him about our cars, I could smell trouble. I knew he'd never be satisfied. I couldn't just say, 'No, we won't rent to you.' Instead I have developed a theory that works out well in practice. I call it finesse versus force.

So I said, 'Look, I think you'll be much happier with Avis, where I know you'll find exactly what you want. I'll be happy to drive you over there.' I did just that and again there were two happy people, a pleased car renter and a relieved me.

In 1974, our way of doing business became so successful that people in other parts of the country asked if we could franchise them.

Today, some 400 Rent-A-Wreck agencies cover the United States and Australia. We are the world's sixth-largest car-rental firm.

Most of the people who drive Rent-A-Wrecks are doing it on their own money instead of expense accounts. They figure they drive a used car at home so why not do the same when travelling and save as much as £100 a week. Today, our cars are only slightly more used than the 'major' firms. In fact, we now offer new cars too. And all of them have been safety checked, run great and now come complete with ashtrays.

But there is one thing I stress to a prospective franchise. 'If money is your only goal, then forget it.' I believe that, in any enterprise, if you make money your god, then the business will never be really successful. For then you're never satisfied; you've put the cart before the horse.

But if a person enjoys filling needs and making people happy, then there's no end to his success and he doesn't have to worry about money. It was all put into one sentence 2,000 years ago by Jesus Christ when he said: 'Whatsoever you would have others do unto you, do so unto them.' It's a very good principle for businessmen too.

I'LL NEVER FORGET

by Calvin Fudge

I thought, if Mr Eli would only say the quality is a little better than it really is, we might get that car yet.

The year I turned seventeen, 1942, had been a bad one for the cotton farmers in southern Arkansas. The boll weevil and heavy rains had taken their toll. The meagre crop had been picked and ginned – all but the last load. On the bright autumn Saturday that we hoisted the last pickings into the wagon to sell, I was troubled about the low price we would get for the crop.

Cotton-selling time meant different things to different people. To some, it meant new shoes, new dresses, a new cooker or money in the bank. To me, it meant *almost* a car. I was in love for the first time, and I had wanted my father to buy a car so I could impress my girl. 'If this had been a normal year for cotton, we could have that car,' my father had said. 'But with this crop ...'

Even with the growing-up problems of a seventeen-year-old boy, I wouldn't have missed today's trip to the gin in El Dorado, five miles away, for anything. I had been going with Mr Eli on these trips ever since I was big enough to sit on the wagon seat beside him.

Mr Eli was a sharecropper on my father's farm, as he had been when my father's father ran the farm. From the time I was three I had been following this old man. He always had time for me. I rode the handles of his plough in the spring as he turned the expectant earth, readying it for seed. I listened tirelessly to his endless versions of Uncle Remus tales. But most of all I enjoyed Mr Eli's stories from the Bible. He always gave his kind admonition that I must be a good boy, honest and true, because the Good Lord wanted me to be.

As far as books and travel were concerned, Mr Eli was unschooled; he could neither read nor write. But he went to church regularly, and his grandson read to him – mostly from the Bible – almost daily. And the years had given him wisdom and patience, two qualities the young seldom understand.

Now I looked sideways at him on the wagon seat as I flapped the reins impatiently across the backs of the old mules.

'Someday we'll haul the cotton to the gin in a big truck, Mr Eli. Or maybe we'll build our own gin. Times can't be bad always.'

He put a wrinkled hand on my knee and grinned. 'Impatience is a boy. Lookin' beyond tomorry is a man. Son, I say you well on the road to bein' a man.' We rode awhile in silence. Then I asked, Mr Eli, 'When you were a boy, did you ever fall in love?'

Once again the thoughtful smile before answering. 'A boy falls in love lots o' times. A man only once.'

'How old do you have to be before you're a man, a real man?'

'It ain't the years, son. It's how, you thinks here,' Mr Eli said, pointing to his head, 'and how you feels here,' indicating his heart. 'When you start thinkin' mo' o' others than yo'self, then you're a man.'

The sun was warm as it neared its zenith. The passing cars went unnoticed as Mr Eli and I sat immersed in our own thoughts. I was remembering what he had said when I wanted to quit school. 'Son, the Lord give you a good mind; it'd be a sin not to use it.' I had complained that school was too hard. 'I s'pect God would help you if you asked.' And when Mr Eli smiled after that remark I expected he was right. Later, it turned out that he was.

While we waited our turn at the gin storehouse, Mr Eli and I prepared to eat the sack lunches my mother had packed for us. I bowed my head because I knew he was going to pray before we ate; he always had, wherever we were – under a tree, in the field.

'Dear Lord,' he prayed, 'thank you for this crop. It ain't the bes' we ever had, but we're thankful. Coulda been worse. Help us git the bes' honest price for it. Please put yo' hand on this fine boy, Lord. Thank you for our daily bread Amen.'

We ate our sandwiches and apples.

When we finished, we drank from the pump spout as we took turns pumping water at the overflowing wooden watering trough.

I set to thinking about selling the cotton. My father had told Mr Eli to sell all of our cotton that was stored here at the gin, now that this was our last crop of the season. Mr Eli had always sold the cotton for the very best price. Mr White, who bought our cotton, seldom tested the fibre of our crop. He always asked Mr Eli about the quality of the fibre and paid him accordingly. I knew the buyer trusted the old man without reservation.

And, I thought, *if Mr Eli would only say the quality is a little better than it really is, we might get that car yet.*

But I knew there wasn't a dishonest bone in the old man, and there would be no use in talking to him about it – even if I had the courage to ask him. But if *I* could sell the cotton! I really did want that car.

Our turn came and we drove the wagon under the giant suction tube. Soon the wagon was empty. Mr Eli put his hand on my shoulder. 'Son, you sell the cotton.'

I was caught off guard. 'B-but –' I stammered.

'You got to start sometime,' he said gently. 'I'm a old man, and I ain't goin' be with you always.'

Mr Eli had never spoken about being old, and I looked at him in surprise. For the first time in my life I saw how really old he was. His hair was as white as the cotton in the bales stacked all around us. The wrinkles on his face and hands were countless. I suddenly had a strange new sense of responsibility.

Mr White came over to us. 'Well, Mr Eli, what kind of crop did you folks have this year?'

'Mr Bob,' Mr Eli said, 'today, my young frien' is sellin'.'

I straightened and stood erect and tried to look important.

'Well, young man?' Mr White said. My heart quickened. Now was my chance to get the good price. Perhaps I'd get that car after all.

'Well, Mr White,' I started. Then I looked at Mr Eli, beaming with pride at me, and my foolish mind went wild with nostalgia. I remembered all the times Mr Eli had spoken about truth and honesty, and how just an hour before, he had prayed for an *honest* price for our crop – and how he had asked God to put his hand on 'this fine boy'. What hit me hardest was the fact that though Mr Eli had taught me with words, more importantly he had *shown* me with his actions.

The examples of his life were standing before me like a panel of judges, waiting to see if I knew right from wrong.

I'd been taught well, not only by my parents but also by this old man whom I knew then to be my finest friend. Hesitantly, I said, 'Mr White, I'm not as good at judging fibre as Mr Eli, so you'd better see for yourself.'

Mr White opened his knife slit the side of a bale of our cotton and pulled out a sample of the short fibre.

The transaction completed, I put the cheque for the cotton into my pocket. Mr Eli and I climbed onto the empty wagon and headed the mules towards home.

We rode in silence. I knew I had done the right thing. Somehow the decision made me feel taller. Older. Mr Eli must have sensed my thoughts, because he said, 'Son, the highes' reward a man gits for his toil is not what he gits in money, but what it makes him. And tellin' the truth is character, and character is mo' important than that cheque in yo' pocket.'

I knew Mr Eli was watching me as I considered what he had just said. Then, resting his hand on my knee, he went on. 'Son, the Lord laid his hand on you today.' He smiled. 'You not a boy anymo'.'

EVERYBODY DOES IT

by Jack Griffin

A boy knows what he's been taught.

When Johnny was six years old, he was with his father when they were caught speeding. His father handed the officer his driver's licence. 'It's okay, son,' his father said as they drove off. 'Everybody does it.'

When he was eight, he was permitted at a family council, presided over by Uncle George, on the surest means to shave points off the income tax return. 'It's okay, kid,' his uncle said. 'Everybody does it.'

When he was nine, his mother took him to his first concert. The ticket agency man couldn't find any seats until his mother discovered an extra ten pounds in her purse. 'It's okay, son,' she said. 'Everybody does it.'

When he was twelve, he broke his glasses on the way to school. His Aunt Francine persuaded the insurance company that they had been stolen and they collected £27. 'It's okay, kid,' she said. 'Everybody does it.'

When he was fifteen, he became right defence on the school football team. His coach showed him how to block and at the same time grab the opposing end by the shirt so the official couldn't see *it*. 'It's okay, kid,' the coach said. 'Everybody does it.'

When he was sixteen, he took his first summer job at the big market. His assignment was to put the over-ripe tomatoes in the

179

bottom of the boxes and the good ones on top where they would show. 'It's okay, kid,' the manager said. 'Everybody does it.'

When he was eighteen, Johnny and a neighbour applied for a college scholarship. Johnny was a marginal student. His neighbour was in the upper three per cent of his class, but he couldn't play right defence. Johnny got the position. 'It's okay,' they told him. 'Everybody does it.'

When he was nineteen, he was approached by an upper class mate who offered the exam answers for three pounds. 'It's okay, kid,' he said. 'Everybody does it.'

Johnny was caught and sent home in disgrace. 'How could you do this to your mother and me?' his father said. 'You never learned anything like this at home.' His aunt and uncle also were shocked.

If there's one thing the adult world can't stand, it's a kid who cheats.

AN AGONIZING DECISION

by Sidney Fields

I saw my son running away.

'Steve,' I asked, 'where are you going?'

He scowled. 'To see Betta,' he said. 'I'll be back soon.'

Betta was his girlfriend. She lived a few streets away, near the park. A nice girl. Good parents.

Steve is my son. Tall, with a broad back, and thick, dark hair. When I held him in my arms, proud of our only son I told my wife: 'He is a gift to the world.' And his mother shared my pride with her soft lovely smile.

For seven years he is our son – and a mystery. We do not know him, Strong and headstrong – and maybe a gifted artist. He works at it in spurts of fury. He will draw a laughing bunch of boys and girls, trees in bloom, kids playing in the snow. Gentle things like that. He has promise.

'Come home early,' his mother said. 'Tomorrow is a school day.'

'I said I'd be back soon, Mum. You worry too much.'

'Before ten-thirty,' I called.

'Okay,' he said and left. It was nine-thirty.

'He'll be all right,' I assured my wife. 'He's just growing up.'

'I don't like those new friends he has,' she said.

We had tried to talk to him about his new friends, but we were in two different worlds. The boys a few blocks away were tough. Steve seemed to want to prove that he was just as tough, that he

181

could hold his own. We tried to talk to him about those friends, about living with purpose. It didn't help.

How do the walls get so high between parents and a child? Steve used to share the music we loved.

We all would go to the park and to the concerts together to hear it. Two years ago he got his own record player, money he saved from a summer job helping commercial artists. He liked his own kind of music, and laughed at ours.

He used to share our faith. A year ago he stopped going to church with us. Maybe we don't know how to make it a real, living thing for him. He just stopped going. It didn't seem good trying to force him.

Every Sunday I ask him, 'Coming with us, Steve?' And he would shake his head. 'You have to be at least thankful.'

'Sure, Dad, I'm very thankful.'

And he began lying – first little lies, then bigger ones.

'Steve, you can't lie and live with yourself,' I said. 'You can't lie no matter how the truth hurts. Lying is stealing with your mind.'

'You're making a big thing out of nothing,' he said. 'If you don't lie now, then you will one day.'

'Never,' I told him. 'No matter how it hurts. I couldn't live with myself.'

My own son, and I don't know him. What could I do or say to show him the meaning of truth? How many parents are there like us?

We went on worrying, and hoping, and praying. At ten thirty my wife said, 'I won't phone Betta's house. He'll tell me I'm treating him like a baby.'

'You lean over backwards not to treat him like a baby,' I said. I went out to find him.

Betta was standing in front of her house. 'Where's Steve?' I asked.

'He went into the park with the other boys a few minutes ago,' she said. 'He told me he'd be back soon to say good night. He'd better hurry. My mother called me twice already.'

'I'll find him,' I said.

I took the first entrance into the park. Why would they go into the park anyway? It was almost eleven. I hurried, searching the darkness for a movement, a sound.

A few seconds later a man's voice suddenly shattered the silence.

'Help! Help!' I rushed towards the noise. Just beyond the glare of a street light four figures bent over a fifth figure on the ground. Racing footsteps were coming down the street. A flashlight swept the darkness. A policeman's whistle shrilled. The four figures leaped up and ran in my direction. As they rushed into the lamplight I saw their faces clearly and my blood froze – one of them was Steve.

Someone came sprinting from behind me, another policeman. He tripped one boy, thudded his foot down hard on his back, grabbed Steve with one hand.

'Stay right here, mister!' he ordered me. The first policeman moved towards us, holding the two other boys. They forced all four to a bench, and made them sit down. One policeman stood behind the bench, the second in front.

I was standing at one end of the bench; Steve sat at the other end. We did not look at each other.

The man who had been on the ground hobbled over to us, cursing. 'They mugged me!' he yelled. 'One of them has my watch.'

The policeman in front of the bench quickly searched all the boys. He found the watch in one boy's pocket. He found a knife in another boy's pocket.

The man who had been mugged looked at them one by one, in a blind, cursing rage. He stared at me.

'Who's this guy?' he asked.

The second policeman pointed to the spot under the light where I had been standing. 'He was there.'

They asked me questions: my name, address, what I did for a living and finally the question that drained the blood from my heart.

'Did you see them?'

I tried to speak. No words came out. My mouth was dry with the taste of ashes. I was trembling. I shut my eyes to shut out the ugliness before me. I couldn't. I was there. My son was there. Three other boys were there. A man who might have been killed was there. I had seen it all.

To myself I said, *No officer. I live just a few streets away. I was just taking a walk. I heard a man yell, help. But I saw nothing. Nothing.*

Steve, you can't lie, and live with yourself . . . it's stealing with your mind . . . You can't . . .

'Did you see them?' the first policeman asked again.

'Look, mister,' the second policeman said. 'This is important. You let a few punks get away with this and they laugh at the law and go on mugging, and worse. Tomorrow it might be your wife or your kid.'

My wife! What would I say to her? Where were the words for that? My mind was in agony, my words came out hoarse: 'I saw them.'

The policeman behind the bench pointed his hand at the first. 'Was this one?'

I nodded. He pointed to the second boy, then the third. I nodded. He reached the end of the bench. I looked away.

'Was this one too?'

I couldn't turn my head towards Steve. I nodded.

'You're not looking at him,' the second policeman said. 'Look at him. Look at him good.'

Steve, you can't lie and live with . . .

My heart was weeping. I was numb with pain.

'Come on over here!' the second policeman ordered Steve. He waved him in front of me with the gun. The policeman behind the bench flashed his light full in Steve's face. I looked up slowly. Steve's eyes were filled with dread.

'Steve,' I said, 'Steve . . .'

'Steve!' the second policeman said. 'You know him!'

'He's my son.'

They were the most painful words I would ever utter.

Both policemen stared. The mugged man's mouth opened in disbelief. Steve glared at me, hate and tears filling his eyes.

'Steve,' I said, 'one day you'll know you can't lie ... Steve!'

He turned his back on me ...

Steve and the other three boys served two years of a three-year sentence. Here is part of a letter Steve sent from jail:

'Dear Dad, I thought about what you did for the thousandth time and hated you for it. But what I see here in prison made a lot of that hatred go. All of the guys here are full of hate – and I don't want to do the same.

'I know now that life has to have truth. Without it, it's no life, here or hereafter.

'You asked me to forgive you for saying those words that terrible night in the park, "He is my son." You wrote to me that those words were not your last words that your last words would have to come from me, from what I make of myself. I ask you and mother to forgive me. I pray God that he will too so the final words will be good words, and you can say, not with pain and shame, but with pride and love, "He is my son."'

WORDS TO GROW ON

by Walter Cronkite

Flirting with Dishonesty

There came a time when I was growing up that I wanted to own a watch. In fact, I had a particular watch picked out, an Ingersoll on display in our local store. It cost a pound. Since I had no money, and no prospects for raising the money quickly, I asked the shop owner if I could take the watch and pay for it little by little. He agreed, and the next day, when my mother happened to come into the store, he casually mentioned the arrangement we'd made.

My mother would have none of it. She was a woman of scrupulous honesty, and to her, I'd taken advantage of another person's willingness to trust me. She paid the shop owner the money and hurried home to confront me.

'Don't you see?' she said. 'Your intentions are honourable, but even you admit you don't know how you're going to earn the money for that watch. There's no outright dishonesty here, but you're flirting with it. It's one of those risky grey areas, Walter. Be careful of grey – it might be grime.'

Then she took the watch and kept it until I earned the money to retrieve it.

Throughout the years since that experience, I've had plenty of reasons to remember my mother's admonition. As a newscaster I've always had to be on guard against grey – a presentation of only half the facts, a story that didn't ring quite true. And there have been such occasions in my personal life as well. One time, for instance, some speculators offered to give me a large parcel of land. There was no suggestion that I talk about their property on the air. They were not being dishonest; they just wanted to be able to say that I owned land in the area that they were trying to promote. But it seemed like a grey area to me. I didn't accept the offer.

I believe that most of the people in this world are honest and want to be honest. But honesty, like all other virtues, requires vigilance. My mother, Helen, knew this. This is what she had in mind as she helped me to stay clear of ambiguity – the grey areas that might be grime.

THAT TOOTHPASTE SMILE

by Austin Colgate

Giving a 'full-pound' was the secret behind a successful empire.

I don't earn my living by soap making like the great-great-grandfather who started our family business. But I try to use the business principle that guided him when the nineteenth century was new.

In 1802, William Colgate, a lad of eighteen, worked alongside his father at the Mather Soap Works in Baltimore. The Colgates were poor, and when Will's father was offered the chance to manage a farm north of New York City, he gladly accepted. The elder Colgates took Will's seven younger brothers and sisters with them, but Will was considered old enough to fend for himself. He was left behind. Disconsolate, fearful, Will's first thought was to run off. As he trudged along a canal-boat towpath, an old neighbour, a canal-boat captain, recognized him.

'Where you heading, Will?' he hailed.

'I don't know,' was the glum response. 'Father says I have to make my own living now.'

'No trouble about that,' said the captain. 'Be sure you start right and you'll get along fine. What can you do?'

'The only trade I know anything about is soap and candle making.'

'Well,' said the old man, 'sooner or later someone will have to be the best soap maker here. It can be you as well as anyone. Let me pray with you.'

The old man prayed earnestly for William and then gave him this advice. 'Be a good man: Give your heart to God. Make an honest soap and give a full pound.'

In those days soap was sold by the pound; unscrupulous makers would short-weight their product or add filler in the form of animal hair, debris, even nails.

Will Colgate returned to his job at the soap works. On finishing his apprenticeship, he got a job at the Slidell Soap Factory in New York. After two years he became business manager, giving a 'full pound' in his product, and his human relationships as well. In 1806 Will founded a tallow chandlery and soap factory in lower Manhattan. Eventually, he expanded the business to include various toiletries, including the famous toothpaste.

Today, I often walk past the Dutch Street address of the original Colgate Company. And I think of how the old captain's advice applies to all of us, no matter whether we sell shoes, repair cars or, as I do, advise on securities. Saint Paul said, 'Be a good workman, one who does not need to be ashamed when God examines your work.'

6

WHEN DREAMS
COME TRUE

*Motivation is when your dreams
put on work clothes.*

Parkes Robinson

THE DREAM THAT WOULDN'T GO AWAY

by George Hunt

Remarkably, I knew I had been shown where those people were and that they were still alive.

Back when I was a young farmer north of Roosevelt, Utah, the news, one cold November morning, reported that a California doctor and his wife were missing on a flight from Custer, South Dakota, to Salt Lake City. As a student pilot, I had just completed my first cross-country flight with an instructor, though I had only twenty solo hours.

Paying close attention to all radio reports on the search, I was very disturbed two days later by a newscast saying that Dr Robert Dykes and his wife, Margery, both in their late twenties and parents of two young children, were not likely to be found until spring – and maybe not even then. They had been missing for four days, and the temperature had been below zero every night. There seemed little chance for their survival without food and proper clothing.

That night before I retired I said a simple prayer for these two people I didn't know. 'Dear God, if they're alive, send someone to them so they will be able to get back to their family.'

After a while I drifted off to sleep. In a dream I saw a red plane on a snow-swept ridge and two people waving for help. I awoke with a start. Was it the Dykeses? What colour *was* their plane? I didn't remember any of the news reports ever mentioning it.

I couldn't get back to sleep for some time. I kept reasoning that because I had been thinking of the couple before falling asleep, it was natural for me to dream of them. When I finally did go to sleep, the dream came again! A red plane on a ridge – but now farther away. I could still see two people waving, and could now see some snow-covered mountain peaks in the background.

I got out of bed and spread out the only air chart I owned. It covered a remote area in Utah – the High Uintas region, along the Wyoming-Utah border. The Dykeses' flight plan presumably had to pass over this range. I was familiar with the rugged terrain, for I had fished and hunted it as a boy. My eyes scanned the names on the chart – Burro Peak, Painters Basin, Kings Peak, Gilbert Peak.

Again I went to bed. And again, incredibly, the dream returned! Now the plane was barely in sight. I could see a valley below. Then it came to me in a flash – Painters Basin and Gilbert Peak! I rose in a cold sweat. It was daylight.

Turning on the news, I found there had been no sign of the plane and the search had been called off. All that day, doing chores around the ranch, I could think of nothing but the Dykeses and my dream. I felt I had been shown where those people were and that they were alive. But who would believe me and what could I do about it? I knew I wasn't really qualified to search for them myself. I knew too that even trying to explain my dream to my flight instructor, a stern taskmaster named Joe Mower, would have me laughed out of the hangar.

I decided to go to our small rural airport anyway. When I arrived, a teenage boy who was watching the place told me Joe had gone to town for the mail. The force that had been nudging me all morning seemed to say, 'Go!' I had the boy help me push an Aeronca plane out. When he asked where I was going, I said, 'To look for the Dykeses.' I gave the plane the throttle and was on my way.

Trimming out, I began a steady climb and headed for Uinta Canyon. I knew what I was doing was unwise, even dangerous, but the danger seemed a small thing compared to what I felt in my heart. As I turned east near Painters Basin, I was beginning to lose faith in my dream; there was no sign of the missing plane. The high winds, downdrafts and rough air were giving me trouble in the small 65-horsepower plane. Terribly disappointed as well as frightened, I was about to turn back when suddenly there it was! A red plane on Gilbert Peak, just as I had seen in my dream.

Coming closer, I could see two people waving. I was so happy I began to cry. 'Thank you, God,' I said over and over again.

Opening the plane's window, I waved at the Dykeses and wigwagged my wings to let them know I saw them. Then I said a prayer to help me get back to the airport safely.

Thirty minutes later I was on the ground. When I taxied up and cut the motor, I gulped, for Joe Mower was there to greet me.

'You're grounded,' he hollered. 'You had no permission to take that plane up.'

'Joe,' I said quickly, 'I know I did wrong, but listen, I found the Dykeses and they need help.'

'You're crazy,' Joe said, and he continued to yell at me. My finding that plane in an hour and a half when hundreds of planes had searched in vain for nearly a week was more than Joe could believe.

Finally I turned away from Joe, went straight for a telephone and did what I should have done in the first place. I called the Civil Air Patrol in Salt Lake City. When they answered, I asked if there had been any word on the Dykeses' plane. They said there was no chance of their being alive now and that the search was ended.

'Well, I've found them,' I said. 'And they're both alive.'

Behind me, Joe stopped shouting at me, his eyes wide and his mouth open. 'I'll round up food and supplies, and the people here will get it to them as soon as possible.' The CAP gave me the go-ahead.

Everyone at the airport went into action. Within one hour we were on our way. A local expert pilot, Hal, would fly in the supplies. I would lead the way in another plane. I wasn't grounded for long.

Back in the air, we headed for the high peaks. Hal's plane was bigger and faster than the Aeronca I was in. He was flying out ahead and above me. When I got to Painters Basin at 11,000 feet, I met the severe downdrafts again. I could see Hal circling above me and knew he was in sight of the downed plane and ready to drop supplies. Since I couldn't go any higher, I turned around.

Back at the airport I joined a three-man ground rescue party, which would attempt to reach the couple by horseback.

Another rescue party had already left from the Wyoming side of the mountains. For the next twenty-four hours our party hiked through fierce winds and six-foot snowdrifts. At 12,000 feet, on a ridge near Gilbert Peak, we stopped. In the distance, someone was yelling. Urging our frozen feet forward, we pressed on, tremendously excited. Suddenly, about ten yards in front of us, the fuselage of a small red plane sat rammed into a snow bank. Nearby, two people flapped their arms wildly.

Charging ahead, we shouted with joy. At about the same time we reached the Dykeses, the other rescue party was coming over the opposite ridge.

After much hugging and thanking, I learned what a miracle the Dykeses' survival was. They had had nothing to eat but a chocolate bar, and their clothing was scant – Mrs Dykes had a fur coat, but her husband had only a mac. The altitude made starting a fire impossible and at night they huddled together in their downed plane, too afraid to go asleep.

'We had all but given up, had even written notes as to who should look after the children,' Mrs Dykes said. Then, turning to me, she said, 'But when we saw your plane, it was the most wonderful thing ... our prayers answered, a dream come true.'

'Yes,' I said, smiling. My dream had occurred for a reason. In order to help give life to two others. Even in the most mysterious of ways, God had shown me he is always there, always listening. He had heard my prayers and the Dykeses' prayers and had answered all of us in his own infallible way.

A GIANT BESIDE OUR HOUSE

by Ron Gullion

As a computer engineer he never really paid any attention to dreams until now.

I'm in our garden on Big Fir Court, gazing up at the mighty 250-foot tree the street is named after. Rising from the corner of our property to the height of a 20-storey building the great white fir dwarfs our home and everything in sight like some ancient giant. It gives the illusion of leaning ominously towards me, creaking and swaying ever so slightly in the rustling wind.

Look! It's not leaning it's falling! It's toppling towards our house, gaining momentum, rushing to meet its shadow, until finally it crumples the roof and splinters through the living room and front bedroom with a sickeningly thunderous roar. I let out a cry. Alison's room!

I awoke in a drenching sweat and sat bolt upright trying to blink away the terrifying vision.

Another nightmare. I slipped out of bed and stole a peek into Alison's room. Our nine-year-old daughter was sleeping peacefully, as was eleven-year-old Heath across the hall. But I couldn't shake the irrational fear until I'd checked. This was not the first time I'd dreamed of such an accident. In another dream I'd seen a giant tree limb tearing loose and slamming down on Heath, leaving him crippled.

As a computer engineer, I deal with quantifiable information. I don't pay much attention to impractical things like dreams. But these nightmares were so vivid and frightening. I eased back into bed next to my wife, Nita, but not before looking out the window at the tree. There it stood, stately and still; its coarse bark ghostly pale in the faint moonlight.

A few nights later I had another dream, this one more puzzling than alarming: I am in our garden and in front of me stands a white angel. The angel has a broken wing. What did all these dreams mean?

Then one day I noticed a twenty-foot dead limb dangling from the fir. We call a dangerous branch like that a widow maker. I remembered the dream about Heath. 'Don't go near that tree,' I warned him.

That Saturday I enlisted a neighbour to help me rope it down. All week I'd worried about the precarious branch and had some other dead limbs removed too.

Why am I so concerned about this tree? I wondered. It's stood here for generations. It even survived the fierce storm of '62.

My nightmares about the tree eventually subsided. Christmas season arrived and Nita and I rushed madly to get our shopping done. More than anything my daughter wanted a Cabbage Patch doll. We scoured the stores with no luck. Everywhere we went it was the same story. 'Sorry,' said the shopkeepers inevitably. 'We sold out our Cabbage Patch dolls weeks ago.'

Finally Nita settled on a handmade rag doll. It was thicker and heavier than the Cabbage Patch version, but there was something about it that caught our fancy. 'Well,' sighed Nita as we paid for it, 'this will have to do.'

'Alison will love it,' I reassured her.

We arrived home to a surprise. Alison had impetuously decided to rearrange her room. She had been talking about it for days, but Nita had implored her to wait until the holiday excitement died down. 'Then I'll help you,' she'd promised.

Instead, Alison had recruited her brother for the task, getting Heath to help drag her heavy bed across the room. 'I just wanted to get it done now, Mummy,' she explained as Nita surveyed the scene with obvious displeasure. 'It's important.' Alison's toys and furniture spilled out into the hall. By bedtime, however, Alison had her room in order again and we could scarcely hide our admiration.

'See?' said Alison knowingly. 'It's not such a big deal.'

Outside I heard the wind whistle through the big fir. A howling blizzard marked Christmas Eve. I drove home from work through swirling snow and pounding winds. I pulled into the driveway, turned up my collar, and hurried inside to get ready for church. Church was not one of my priorities even under the best circumstances, and on a night like this I didn't want to be anywhere but inside my house, Christmas Eve or not. But I'd promised.

At the service with Nita and the kids, I felt strangely detached as I hunched in the pew with my arms folded tightly, thinking about whether I even believed that God was a part of my life. I had been raised in church but that was a long time ago. Now I certainly didn't feel any 'tidings of comfort and joy'. God may have created the world and all its wonders, but I didn't see where that had much to do with my life. If God was real, he was much too remote for me to have faith in. We arrived home late, and the wind and snow stung our faces as we walked up the driveway. Heath and Alison rushed inside to turn on the Christmas tree lights From our bay window the blue lights cast a peaceful glow across the snowy garden I draped my arm around Nita and led her in.

Wrapping paper flew as the children tore into a few early presents, and Nita and I settled back on the couch to view the happy chaos. Nita had turned the tree into a work of art. The crowning touch was a glorious blonde angel perched high at the top. 'It looks like Alison,' I said.

Alison was so delighted with her big new doll that she granted it the honour of accompanying her to bed. 'Told you she'd love it,' I reminded Nita as we climbed under the covers. The moaning wind lulled us to sleep.

ROAR! The explosive sound jolted the house. I hadn't been asleep long, and my startled, half-awake mind tried to separate fantasy from reality. The dream again, I thought. But then I sat bolt upright, and suddenly I knew. This was no dream. This time my nightmare was real. The tree really had fallen on our house!

I leapt out of bed and raced across the hall to Alison's room. 'Daddy, help!' she was calling frantically. 'I'm stuck!'

I couldn't budge the door. It was jammed shut 'Oh, my God,' I whispered. 'Don't move, honey!' I shouted through the door. 'We'll get you out.' I grabbed a torch and told Nita to call for help. 'I'll see if I can get to her from outside.'

I was horrified to find the tree filling the front hall, branches whipping in the gale. I stumbled through the family room to a side door. Outside I nearly collided with the trunk, propped up on its giant ball of roots, which had been torn from the earth. It looked prehistoric. I crawled underneath as the rough bark tore at my robe and ripped my flesh. The wind sliced through me. Above the din I heard the distant wail of sirens.

Groping my way to Alison's window I aimed the flashlight beam inside and wiped the icy snow from my eyes. All I could see were branches, tattered insulation and hunks of ceiling strewn about the trunk. Somewhere buried beneath the tree was my daughter, crying faintly, 'Daddy! Daddy!'

Someone was standing beside me. 'Alison! This is Captain McCullough of the fire brigade,' he called. 'Your daddy's with me. Can you move at all?'

'I think I can move my arm,' came a brave little voice.

'Good. Push your hand up as high as you can.'

Tiny fingers wriggled up through the debris. I breathed a tentative sigh of relief. Firemen rushed to set up lights and heat lamps. They fastened a plastic tarpaulin over the rescue area. Captain McCullough turned to me and said quietly, 'This isn't going to be easy, Mr Gullion.'

As I huddled with Nita and neighbours looked after Heath, a terrifying game of pick-up-sticks slowly unfolded. The night air was filled with the roar of chainsaws and the reek of fir pitch as rescuers cut away at the tree and cautiously removed branches as they went. A slight shift of any debris could spell disaster.

Bit by bit they chipped away at the wreckage until, after an hour, Alison's head and shoulders emerged. Her right leg appeared to be crushed under the tree. A fallen two-by-six rafter clamped down on her torso. We could see Alison's new doll squeezed between her chest and the rafter. Apparently she'd fallen asleep clutching it.

McCullough shook his head grimly and called a halt to the work. 'We can't risk it,' he said. 'Show me the crawl space.' Moments later he shone his torch on the area under Alison's room. Huge branches a half foot in diameter pierced the floor and stabbed the ground beneath. Again McCullough shook his head. 'We can't cut away the floor without disturbing the tree. And that tree must not shift.'

The subzero wind had intensified. Hours had passed and now there was the threat of Alison succumbing to hypothermia. Neighbours rushed in warm blankets and hot-water bottles. A paramedic put his wool cap on Alison's head. But I could see she was drifting, her big eyes fluttering. Once or twice her head rolled back. If we didn't get her leg out soon, the surgeons might have to amputate it to free her.

Only one option was left: Lift the tree.

A crane was out of the question. In this wind it would be too unstable. But McCullough had called a towing company that used giant air bags to gently right overturned trucks. 'It's a gamble,' he warned me. 'But we've run out of options.'

Huge rubber bags were packed under the tree. A compressor roared to life. Slowly the bags filled with air and swelled against the great fir. Despite the blizzard, I could see sweat bead up on McCullough's tensed brow. My hands trembled as Nita buried her head in my chest, afraid to look.

Suddenly, I heard myself praying to the God whose very existence I'd doubted just hours earlier. You would have thought I'd be ashamed to ask for his help now, but something told me I must. 'Please, Lord,' I begged. 'Spare her life. I believe you are here.'

The shriek of the compressor was deafening. The bags bulged like great billows, but at first nothing gave.

Then there was movement! Inch by agonizing inch, the tree was lifted. A cry rose from the crowd as paramedics rushed to free Alison and whisk her to a waiting ambulance. Nita and I jumped in with her, and we roared off. Alison smiled weakly. 'I'll be okay now, Daddy,' she whispered, still grasping her new doll.

That overstuffed doll, it turned out, was possibly just enough of a cushion between the fallen two-by-six rafter and Alison's chest to have saved her life. The doctors confirmed that she would recover. And Alison's leg was only broken, not crushed.

Christmas Day, Heath and I kicked through the rubble of our house. I'd been thinking about that desperate prayer I'd said, thinking about it a lot. In Alison's room I saw that the bulk of the fir had landed near the southeast wall – right where her bed had been before she'd impulsively moved it. On the trunk directly over where Alison lay when the tree came crashing through, I noticed a wide scar from a recently cut branch – one of those I'd felt such urgency to remove after my dream. That branch might have killed her.

Had God been trying to warn me all along about the tree? To protect us? Had I been blind to God's ways?

In the snow outside what used to be our living room I found the angel from our Christmas tree, the one that looked like Alison. Its wing was broken, just as the angel's wing in my dream had been. As I brushed it off and held it up, Heath came running. 'Dad, Dad!' He grabbed the angel. 'I've seen this before! In a dream! Angels with broken wings just like this one!'

Dreams. Does God speak to us through them? This much I myself can say: Alison is safe and well. And God is, and always has been, watching over my family.

THE PIN

by Mary Rosco

It's often the little things that mean so much.

I suppose none of us know the meaning of dreams. But I know what prayers can do. I was working the three-to-eleven shift at my local hospital, when a patient I was feeding asked, 'Why don't you have a little pin like the other nurses?'

'I do,' I said, reaching to show him the golden, wreath-shaped R.N. pin on my collar, one of my proudest possessions. It had been given to me when I graduated from nursing school, and it stood for years of hard work and study.

But now when I looked down, the pin was gone. I knew I had pinned it to myself before I left the house. I looked everywhere for it. A colleague and I searched through all the linens and bedside equipment but found nothing. I even took a mop and dusted under the beds.

At home I turned the place upside down. No pin. Of course I could replace it, but a substitute would never mean as much.

That night, as lay in bed, I prayed that the Lord would help me find it.

Soon I was asleep. In the deep of night I had a dream. I dreamed that I got out of bed, put on my slippers and ran downstairs and out the door to a puddle of water in front of the house. And in this puddle was my pin.

The next morning I awoke disappointed. 'It was only a dream,' I muttered to myself. 'A worthless dream.' But as my head cleared,

I seemed to hear a voice saying, *No, it's more than a dream. Go and see.*

I put on my slippers and walked out to the road in front of our house, and found there a puddle of water. I placed my hand into the brown water. In a moment I held in my hand an answered prayer.

RECURRING DREAM

by June Davis

A disturbed night saves a life.

My mother had been haunted by the same dream for five nights in a row. She described it to me as I took her to the hospital for an operation to relieve a slipped disc.

'It's snowing,' she said. 'In the distance I can see headlights approaching. When they come close, I recognize a hearse. It stops in front of me. A door opens and the driver motions me inside . . .'

Against her wishes, I told Mum's doctors and nurses about the dream so they would be sensitive to her fears about the operation.

Before dawn on the day of her surgery the snow began to fall. At 7.15 I went to her hospital room to be with her while she was prepared. An orderly came in and I helped him get Mum on the trolley. We were waiting at the lift when a nurse hurried up. 'The surgery has been cancelled,' she said.

Finally, I was able to reach our doctor to find out what was going on. 'Well, I woke up during the night and couldn't go back to sleep,' he said. 'Something was bothering me. I looked outside and saw the snow. I thought about your mother's dream. I called the hospital and ordered a second electrocardiogram. It caught a heart condition that didn't show up on the first one. The lab called the anaesthetist and he cancelled the procedure.'

The doctor hesitated and took a deep breath.

'If your mother had had the anaesthetic, well . . .'

Later I found out what he did not say then. Under anaesthesia, Mum would have been in grave danger of dying of heart failure.

A DREAM COME TRUE

by Norman Vincent Peale

Persistence made it happen for a young woman with all the odds stacked against her.

A big thought can be one of the strongest forces in the world. I was impressed with that idea all over again when I heard the story of Mary Crowe.

Young Mary was washing her father's overalls one day when the big thought struck her.

In her mind she saw herself graduating from college in cap and gown, accepting her diploma, ready to start a career.

Since Mary came from a low-income family, her dream seemed out of sight. There would never be enough money to send Mary to college. Besides, no member of her family had ever gone to college.

But Mary held on to that thought. In secondary school she studied hard, and spoke freely of her dream to teachers and friends. When her final day at school came, her principal called her into his office.

'I have an envelope for you,' he said.

It contained a scholarship to a nearby college. The power of a thought had produced its first dividend. But the scholarship could cover only part of her college expenses. Mary took every part-time job she could find and became a waitress, a housemaid, a cook.

Mary's dream came true when she graduated from college. Then she took a course in insurance. When she presented herself to a local insurance company for a job, she was turned down. She applied again. The answer was no. She kept going back until the manager, to get rid of her, snapped. 'All right, here's a rate book and a desk. But I can't give you a drawing account or any secretarial help.'

Twenty-five years later Mary Crowe's associates in that company gathered at a special dinner in her honour, recognizing her for her outstanding achievements as an insurance saleswoman.

'Each of us is constantly in a state of becoming,' she said, giving her formula for success. 'And through enthusiasm, prayer and faith you can become what you think. Not that your life will be without problems. But along the way problems will be overcome. Ask and believe; dream and believe; work and believe.'

A VOICE IN THE BLIZZARD

by Vance Thurston

I lay there, snow covering my freezing body. I was so tired and defeated I just wanted to sleep.

Bitter cold had made life a struggle on the plains of northeastern Montana. Darkness was rapidly approaching and snow crunched beneath my insulated boots. I held my hand to my face, blocking the raw wind. Lady, my border collie, huddled close to my feet as she would when a storm was coming in. After another day spent coaxing frozen machinery to run and feeding cattle, I felt weary all over.

I thought about going straight home while there was still light. My own place was more than a mile south from the ranch where I worked. Since the road was blocked by eight-foot-high drifts, I had been travelling back and forth by snowmobile. But my wife, Mary, was working the night shift at the hospital and wouldn't be home for dinner. So when Charlie, one of the ranch owners, offered to cook, I decided to stay and eat with him.

After supper I trudged out to the shop to fix a broken weld on the loader tractor so it wouldn't hold us up in the morning. I didn't think it would take long, but nothing had gone right that day.

I lost track of time. Finally, the increasing howl of the wind caught my attention. Concerned, I tried to open the shop door to look outside, but a drift was blocking it. I struggled to push the door open and a blast of snow hit me in the face. The ranch house was difficult to see even though it was only 150 feet away. The storm blocked any moonlight, and drifts made the short walk difficult. After reaching the house I scraped ice off the thermometer. It had already dropped to 28 below zero.

'Better stay here tonight,' Charlie suggested. 'You can sleep on the couch.' But I felt compelled to go home and make sure the heat was working in our house. As I put on my winter gear, face mask and goggles, I told Charlie, 'I'll follow the fence line home instead of cutting across the pasture.' After all, I had spent more than thirty years in Montana; I could certainly handle bad weather. Lady held back as I urged her out the door into the heightening blizzard.

It was so cold that the track on the snowmobile was frozen, I finally got it started, and Lady dutifully climbed into her usual spot on the seat in front of me. I manoeuvred around a large drift that covered a corner post. It took a minute to find the fence in the swirling blackness. Reassured, I worked my way along, reminding myself to stay as close to the fence as possible.

Out on the open plain the blizzard grew with frightening intensity. Snow swirled crazily in the headlight. I could no longer see the front runners. My goggles iced over and when I tried to clean them they filled with snow. Hunching closer to the wind shield, I hugged the fence line.

Suddenly the snowmobile lurched. I fought for control as Lady scrambled on the seat. When I looked back, the fence line was gone.

'It's still there,' I reassured myself. 'I've just drifted to the right.' Slowly I turned left. Nothing. I kept turning, expecting to bump into the fence at any moment. Making a fist in my leather mitt, I attempted to warm my numbing fingertips. I decided to travel in a slow circle, concentrating on keeping the snowmobile upright as I continued my way in the unknown darkness.

Nothing – except the moaning wind. I tried what I thought was a larger circle. I couldn't make sense of what was happening. Was this the first sign of hypothermia? The windchill was inescapable. I was freezing. How much time did I have?

Lady looked like an ice-covered porcupine. She stared at me with a bewildered expression as if to ask, 'What are we doing?'

I considered turning her loose to see if she could find the way home. But how would we be able to keep track of each other in this screaming hell of ice? I knew I could not expect rescue from Charlie because I had the only working snowmobile.

Hugging Lady for comfort, I forced my mind to reason. If only I could find the fence line. But how?

In desperation I said a rusty Sunday school prayer. That seemed to help me, so I got more personal. 'Dear God,' I prayed, 'I am in a heap of trouble. Please help me.' Slowly an idea began to form: Use the snowmobile light for a beacon and search for the fence.

Turning the light on high, I got off the snowmobile and started to push my way through the waist-deep snow. After a few steps the wind drowned out all sound of the running engine. If the engine died, the light would too. I forced myself forward as Lady stumbled in my tracks. I tried to carry her, but I didn't have the strength. We struggled on until the light was a dim glow behind us. Nothing. We turned around, drifts already burying our tracks.

When we got back, the snowmobile engine compartment was filling with snow so I turned the sled upwind and tried to speed the engine. When I squinted into the storm, snow collected on my eyelashes and froze my eyes shut. There was nothing to do but plunge forward in another direction. I forced them open and leaned against the wind. Where were we? Nothing made sense. There were miles of prairie and I could find no landmarks. Again we returned to the snowmobile.

The engine was barely running. How much longer could it last? Reluctantly, we cast out again on foot. Glancing back at the fading light I fell face-forward. I lay there, snow covering my freezing body. I was so tired and defeated I just wanted to sleep.

I thought about Mary and wanted to tell her how much I loved her. I thought about our daughter and wondered how she would grow up. 'Dear God,' I prayed, 'help me live!'

Lady nuzzled my face. I spat the snow out of my mouth and struggled to my feet. Then, above the roar of the storm, a voice, as in a hallucination seemed to say, 'Just a little farther'. Was I dreaming things? The wind mocked me as if to answer, 'Your mind is going'. And yet the voice was so compelling that somehow I pushed myself forward. Again I fell, but this time I had tripped on something. Digging frantically I came up with a strand of barbed wire that led to a fence post hidden under the snow.

I nursed the snowmobile back to the wire and followed it. My pockets were filling with snow and I was losing hope when the wire rose out of the snow and became a visible fence. Still I wasn't sure. The wind was moving drifts, changing the landscape before my eyes. I groped on.

The fence had ended! A post with an old piece of rope flapping in the wind marked the end of the line. We seemed so close – but to what? Lady was staring in a distinct direction, her head slightly cocked. Was it the ranch? My teeth chattered, and fear seemed to swirl in the wind. But again I heard the voice: 'Just a little farther.' Was it my imagination?

I squeezed the throttle and the snowmobile went forward. Suddenly, we pitched to a stop. I realized where we were. We had collided with the posts of the ranch-yard cattle guard. A moment later I could see the yard light swaying violently in the wind. We were going to make it!

Lady was mighty glad to be back at the ranch and so was I. Charlie thawed me out with a lot of coffee, but I didn't feel much like talking. I had been gone only two hours, but it had felt like an eternity. I went to bed and Lady slept close by me.

Later the next day, when the storm finally broke, I went outside to figure out how I had become so lost. My almost-fatal error seemed unbelievable in the light of day. While leaving the yard and swinging around the huge mound of snow, I had lost my sense of direction and started down the wrong fence line. That fence went out towards the horizon and disappeared into the endless drifts. I shuddered. How amazing it was that I had found that wire – my lifeline – under those mounds of snow!

As I thought about the voice, I felt mighty grateful I was back at work and able to feed the cows that day.

Things have changed since then. The old fence has been torn down, and my dear dog Lady lies buried beside the creek. I still fall short at times, but I take comfort in knowing we are children of God, loved and cared for even in our darkest hours. I still remember my prayer in the blizzard and how much I wanted to live. When I remember the voice – 'Just a little farther' – I feel at peace. I was hopelessly lost in a blizzard when the grace of God led me home.

HEAVEN IS FOR DANCING

by Catherine Marshall

Bill and Jean wondered how to tell her about her Nana's death. The five-year-old would surely be heartbroken.

Sara Brown, age five, has dark, naturally curly hair, eyes like shiny brown buttons, a rosebud mouth and a low-pitched voice. A blur of bursting vitality and motion, Sara could never sit still for long in anyone's lap – unless, of course, that lap belonged to her grandmother, Louise Brown, whom she called 'Nana'.

Nana, sturdy in build, belying her eighty-three years, with iron-grey hair and lively eyes in a vivacious face, could always be counted on for a story – from a book or from memory. After all, Sara's Nana had been a first-rate teacher for many years.

The two of them would sit cuddled close together in a certain wing chair in the Browns' two-century-old farmhouse. The story Sara asked for over and over was the tale of the 'turkey-gobbler' who had swallowed a child's ring. For Sara, the suspense hung on one question: Would the turkey choke to death?

A very sensitive child, Sara could not bear to see any animal or person hurt. Death was a calamity beyond her comprehension. But the turkey story had such a happy ending! The ring was recovered when the gobbler was held brashly upside down and the ring shaken and stroked out of his long neck. 'He spitted it up,' in Sara's words, and she would laugh and laugh with glee at the funny sight this presented to her mind.

Last winter Louise dislocated a knee, aggravating very painful arthritis. A systemic infection followed, and it invaded the blood-stream. After weeks of hospitalization, Louise came home, confined to a wheelchair, able to take only a few small steps. The doctor's verdict to the family: the end was not far distant.

Louise had lived a long, useful and full life. She was not afraid of death and had always made a point of telling Sara, her only grandchild, how much she looked forward to the joyful reunion with her husband, her mother and father, her four brothers and two sisters who had preceded her into the next life.

But even with this preparation, Jean and Bill Brown, Sara's parents, were troubled. Louise's death would be devastating to their small daughter. So in prayer, they asked for help. The petition was, 'Lord Jesus, please don't let our little girl be hurt. Let this experi-ence be one that will teach her what you want her to know about death and immortality.'

On a Tuesday night, Sara came bursting into her parents' room in the middle of the night. 'A dream woke me up,' she whispered.

Her mother took Sara back to her own bed and crawled in with her. 'Do you want to tell me about the dream?'

'Well, maybe a little bit. I dreamed that Nana was taken up out of her bed . . .' Since Sara seemed reluctant to share more, her mother reassured her that Nana was still in her bed, and both of them drifted off to sleep.

The next morning began normally. The nurse, whom the Browns had employed to care for Louise during the day, arrived. Bill left for work in Washington, and Jean took Sara to playschool on her way to the office.

At 9.30, while the nurse was changing her bed, Louise was sitting in a chair. All at once she sighed and quietly bowed her head. Her life on earth was ended.

The nurse called Jean Brown, and she returned home imme-diately. Bill drove home from Washington.

One moves mechanically at such a time. Contact the local mortuary . . . decisions about the funeral . . . and Sara would soon

214

be back from playschool. Bill and Jean wondered how to tell her about her Nana's death. The five-year-old would be heartbroken. That afternoon when Sara got home her parents took her into the garden. Though it was early February, the day was glorious, warm and sunshiny. Then Sara's father had a sudden inspiration – a divine inspiration. The dream! Sara's dream held the key!

'Honey, tell us again about your dream last night.'

There was a moment of pensiveness. Then Sara brightened, 'Oh, yes! Nana was standing in the air above her bed, dancing, like this.' She stepped back to demonstrate with exuberant twists, turns and pirouettes. 'And Nana's back and legs didn't hurt anymore – not a single bit!'

Her father fought back the tears. 'You know what, Sara? Last night in your dream, God whispered a secret to you before anybody else in the whole world knew. The secret was that today he was going to take Nana up to be with him. She's dancing with the angels in Heaven right now.'

A series of expressions crossed the little girl's face. Then to her parents' surprise, Sara began to laugh and clap and dance some more. She rushed into the house to telephone several of her friends, eagerly sharing the glad tidings that her Nana could walk and even dance now in her new life.

Remembering their prayer request weeks earlier, the Browns stood there marvelling. 'To think,' there was wonder in Jean's voice, 'that God would care that much about one little girl!'

Later that evening some neighbours dropped over; bringing along their seven-year-old daughter. Both sets of parents noticed that the two children were huddled together in the next room, laboriously writing something.

When the guests had gone, Sara handed her mother a piece of paper. With assistance, she had scrawled these exact words to go to her Nana: 'I love you and hope you feel good in heaven.'

Nana is free from pain and doing fine, while some of us earth-bound creatures are once again amazed at the way of a loving heavenly Father. He singled out a little child through whom to pour a special revelation. We know that Heaven is for dancing!

WHERE TO FIND HELP

Having read some of our stories may encourage you to think about your own struggles. If you would like further help on your life journey, here is a list of agencies who may be able to help:

British Association for Counselling
1 Regent Place
Rugby
Warks CV21 2PJ
01788-550899

Families Anonymous (Advice on family problems and drug abuse)
Unit 37
Dodington and Rollo Community Association
Charlotte Despard Avenue
London SW11 5JE
020-7498-4680

ACET (AIDS Advisers)
Central Office
PO Box 3693
London SE15 2BS
020-8780-0400

AGE Concern
Astral House
1268 London Road
London SW16 4ER
020-8679-8000

CRUSE Bereavement Care
Cruse House
126 Sheen Road
Richmond
Surrey TW9 1UR
020-8940-4818

MIND (Advice on Mental Health)
020-8522-1728
0345-660-163

Relate (Marriage and Relationship Advice)
Herbert Gray College
Little Church Street
Rugby
CV21 3AP
01788-573-241

The Institute of Family Therapy (Therapeutic work with families and couples)
24–32 Stephenson Way
Euston
London NW1 2HX
020-7391-9150

The Samaritans (General Help-line)
0345-909-090
jo@samaritans.org

Survivors of Sexual Abuse
020-7890-4732

Book One in the Long Hot Soak series.

A Long Hot Soak

Over 50 stories to warm the heart and inspire the spirit

Edited by Chris Gidney

Immerse yourself in the wit and wisdom of this inspirational new book. It presents a heart warming medley of inspiring true-life stories. Movingly told, these pieces are a spiritual tonic to bring comfort and strength to the reader. These true stories are drawn from the lives of ordinary people – telling of fears conquered, loneliness broken and of the power of faith and love. With over fifty stories, this book is sure to tug at the heart strings and motivate the reader with its inspirational, upbeat messages.

Softcover: 0-002-74056-7

Pick up a copy at your favorite bookstore!

Another Long Hot Soak
Book Two

Over 50 Stories to Warm the Heart and Inspire the Spirit

Edited by Chris Gidney

When the daily grind is getting you down, nothing beats a nice, warm bath with a good book. The stories in this collection do for the soul what a hot soak does for the body: cleanse, relax and refresh.

Another Long Hot Soak – Book Two offers more than fifty true-life stories to comfort and inspire. In this poignant, heartwarming collection, an unwanted child finds a mother and a home. A young woman renews her love for her dying brother. A sailor adrift at sea chooses faith over fear. These are the accounts of real people from all walks of life who have faced every kind of circumstance – the routine, the remarkable, the uncanny, the tragic and even the humorous. Some, in the face of betrayal, have shown astonishing forgiveness and love. Others have stared death in the face and emerged with a deeper sense of purpose. Many have encountered a power greater than themselves that guided their decisions, empowered their actions and engineered outcomes beyond their own ability.

Written in the style of its popular predecessor, *A Long Hot Soak*, this book is a spiritual tonic to bring encouragement and strength in the ups and downs of life.

Softcover: 0-310-25176-1

Pick up a copy at your favorite bookstore!

ZONDERVAN™

GRAND RAPIDS, MICHIGAN 49530 USA

WWW.ZONDERVAN.COM

Book Four Features More
Inspirational True-Life Stories!

Another Long Hot Soak
Book Four

Over 50 Stories to
Warm the Heart and
Inspire the Spirit

Edited by Chris Gidney

Another selection of the most heartwarming true-life stories of courage
and inspiration. This new collection is
drawn from the lives of ordinary
people – telling of fears conquered,
loneliness broken and the power of faith and love.

Movingly told, these short pieces are a spiritual tonic to
bring comfort and strength in the ups and downs of life.
There are over fifty stories here to tug at the heart-strings
and satisfy the reader with encouragement and hope in the
everyday struggle of life.

Softcover: 0-310-25178-8

Pick up a copy at your favorite bookstore!

GRAND RAPIDS, MICHIGAN 49530 USA

WWW.ZONDERVAN.COM

Another Long Hot Soak

BOOK THREE